MORE PRAISE FOR

Pilgrimage into the Last Third of Life

Wisdom is not relegated to any age. *Pilgrimage into the Last Third of Life* explores many facets of aging, particularly its benefits, challenges, and opportunity for satisfying resolution. With increased longevity and significant numbers of people entering the third and final phase of life, there is a historical opportunity available where accrued collective wisdom can change the world for the better. This book offers a most relevant and important perspective on aging and its meaningful purpose beyond legacy leaving.

> ANGELES ARRIEN, PhD, Cultural Anthropologist
> Author of *The Second Half of Life*

The spiritual streams of life seem to swell and flow more fully in the later years. And, although the later years can provide more time for dwelling on the things of the spirit, most adults need help in their search for the deep meanings of life. Thibault and Morgan, in this thoughtful book of meditations and personal revelations, provide wisdom and insight into spiritual growth that is readily available for all adults in the Last Third of life.

> DR. RICHARD H. GENTZLER JR.
> Director, Center on Aging and Older Adult Ministries
> General Board of Discipleship, The United Methodist Church

This devotional guide *is* for those willing to look at aging and to mine its spiritual depths. It *is also* for those unwilling to look aging in the face but who would dare to search for buried treasure.

> KARL A. NETTING, MDiv
> Hospice Chaplain

The dynamic duo of Jane Thibault and Richard Morgan has done it again! *Pilgrimage into the Last Third of Life* is a relevant guidebook to equip each generation to compassionately understand and richly walk through the Last Third of life. This book will become a well-used resource for all who work in the aging community.

Robin Dill
Director of Grace Arbor, the Congregational Respite Ministry
First United Methodist Church Lawrenceville, Georgia
Author of *Walking with Grace*

I like this little volume because the chapters are short and the advice is so practical. It will be helpful to family members, caregivers, and pastors as well. Thanks to Jane and Richard for making their experiences available to many.

J. Roy Stiles
Retired pastor, Louisville, Kentucky

Pilgrimage into the Last Third of Life is transparent, inspiring, and deeply spiritual. The pilgrimage that Jane and Richard reflect upon invites us to enter a reflection on who we are in the later stage of life. This image of pilgrimage conveys mercy, compassion, forgiveness, and strong relationships. The Last Third of Life involves embracing abundant life with Jesus. It is about slowing down and welcoming creative opportunities for contemplation in life. Let us enter the later stage of life with hope.

Brother Wayne J. Fitzpatrick, MM, MA, MS
Director of Life Long Formation and Continuing Education
Maryknoll Fathers and Brothers, Maryknoll, New York

PILGRIMAGE

into the

Last Third *of* Life

7 GATEWAYS TO
SPIRITUAL GROWTH

Jane Marie Thibault

Richard L. Morgan

UPPER
ROOM BOOKS®
NASHVILLE

PILGRIMAGE INTO THE LAST THIRD OF LIFE
7 Gateways to Spiritual Growth
© 2012 by Jane Marie Thibault and Richard L. Morgan
All rights reserved.

The Upper Room Web site: http://www.upperroom.org

Cover design: Bruce Gore/Gorestudio.com
Cover photo: Stan Navratil/All Canada Photos/Getty Images

LIBRARY OF CONGRESS CATALOGING-IN-PUBLICATION DATA
Thibault, Jane M. (Jane Marie), 1946–
  Pilgrimage into the last third of life : 7 gateways to spiritual growth / by Jane Marie Thibault, Richard L. Morgan.
    p. cm.
  ISBN 978-0-8358-1117-0—eISBN 978-0-8358-1122-4
1. Older Christians—Religious life—Meditations. 2. Aging—Religious aspects—Christianity—Meditations. 3. Spiritual formation—Medita-tions.
I. Morgan, Richard Lyon, 1929– II. Title.
  BV4580.T484 2012
  248.8'5—dc23
      2011053104

Printed in the United States of America

Contents

Prayer for Aging

ALL GRACIOUS GOD, You have given me all I am and have,
and now I give it back to You to stand under Your will alone.
In a special way I give You these later years of my life.

I am one of those called by You into old age, a call not given to all,
not given to Jesus, not given to most in our world today.
I humbly ask You, grace me deeply in each aspect of that struggle.

As my physical eyesight weakens,
may the eyes of my faith strengthen,
that I may see You and Your Love in everything.
As my hearing fails, may the ears of my heart
be more attentive to the whisper of Your gentle voice.
As my legs weaken and walking becomes more difficult,
may I walk more truly in Your paths,
knowing all the while that I am held in the embrace of Your love.
As my mind becomes less alert and memory fades
may I remain peaceful in You,
aware that with You there is no need for thought or word.
You ask simply that I be there, with You.

And should sickness overtake me and I be confined to bed,
may I know myself as one with Your Son as he offers his life for
the salvation of the world.

Finally, as my heart slows a little after the work of the years,
may it expand in love for You and all people.
May it rest secure and grateful in Your loving Heart
until I am lost in You, completely and forever.
Amen.

"Prayer for Aging" by Sr. Moya Hanlen, fdnsc, (Australia) Adapted by Ministry of the Arts,
www.ministryofthearts.org

PREFACE
A Word to Our Readers

*T*HE FIRST QUESTION found in old religious instruction books published by many Christian denominations asks, Who made you? Answer: God made me. The second question: Why did God make you? Answer: To know, love, and serve God on this earth and (at the end of life) to be with God and enjoy God forever in heaven. In *Pilgrimage into the Last Third of Life: 7 Gateways to Spiritual Growth*, a book of short meditations, we offer thoughts about some of the best ways we have found to know, love, serve, and enjoy God and one another in the Last Third of life. We define the Last Third loosely as the time between sixty and ninety or seventy and one hundred, which includes people the aging specialists label the "Young Old" and the "Old Old." This unique time offers highly significant challenges—both spiritual and secular.

The challenges and tasks of people in the First Third of life primarily revolve around growth, development, and exploration of life's possibilities. It's an exciting time of life, full of promise. The tasks of the Second Third—the years thirty-five to sixtyish are, for the most part, somewhat more stable. Most of us find ourselves in the workforce with a focus on family and career, even though life and its demands change constantly. During this period of time, we come into maturity and rise to the height of our greatest personal and social power. The years from sixty to ninety-plus relate a different story. The events of these years are so unpredictable for individuals that the theme of the 2009 American Society on Aging conference in Las Vegas was "The Gamble of Aging." It *is* a gamble because, unlike the earlier years when most of us don't have to worry about decline of health and impaired functional abilities, in the Last Third, physical and mental health will predict and define our quality of life from now until death. We find the only clue to our health by looking to our ancestors—how long did they live and what diseases did they miss? Even these variables give just a hint, not a prediction.

Today a sixty-three-year-old person can be the CEO of a company one day and diagnosed with stage 4 colon cancer the next. An eighty-five-year-old can be given two new knees and a new heart valve and run in the next Senior marathon. An eighty-year-old woman can look twenty years younger while a seventy-year-old can look ninety. When two people who look alike come together to the University of Louisville Geriatric Clinic, where I (Jane) have worked for thirty-one years, I never assume they are siblings; more often than not they are mother (ninety) and daughter (seventy)! Because of the vast differences in the way people age, this book attempts to address the spiritual concerns of both the hale and the frail, whatever the chronological age.

In addition to using the term *Last Third*, we also speak of 7 Gateways. Gateways refer to the variety of time-tested, tried and true ways in which we can open ourselves to God and to the abundant life God constantly offers us. We chose the number seven because it symbolizes completion, perfection. In her book *Interior Castle*, Saint Teresa of Ávila wrote of "seven mansions" of the soul that we pass through to open ourselves to union with God.

It is one thing to tap into our knowledge base and life experience to advise other persons. It is quite another to use our own struggles, victories, and failures for the benefit of others. The former allows us to stay safely at the outer gates of the intellect;

the latter demands deep (and often painful) introspection and a willingness to share personal thoughts and experiences. In our previous books, written individually and together, we have shared what we have learned from our personal and professional lives. However, this book, *Pilgrimage into the Last Third of Life: 7 Gateways to Spiritual Growth*, takes a more intimate approach. Here we share our past and current struggles with our aging selves. We dig deep into our lives' realities to mine what may help us and others experience the abundant life that Jesus promises—even unto old-old age with its probable limitations.

In this book we bare our souls once again by presenting ourselves to you using the image of "aging bookends." The bookend named Jane—at sixty-five—is in the first class of Baby Boomers, new to the experience of the Last Third of life (even though, as a clinical gerontologist, she has been thinking, learning, and teaching about it for over thirty years). Jane will share her thoughts and fears of what the future could hold. The bookend named Richard—at eighty-three—is a well-seasoned explorer of the Last Third as well as a long-term teacher of aging issues. He will look back at what has been and forward to what might be in his own life.

You may find that we have sometimes chosen the same scripture passage but present different perspectives. We have tried to express different ideas while acknowledging that sometimes ideas need to be stated more than once.

We have written our reflections in God's light. That is, we look at our aging selves and note secular society's common interpretation of the experiences we share. We then examine how viewing those experiences through the eyes of faith can transform them. We might even be tempted to ask, "How would an *old* Jesus view this situation? What would an *old* Jesus do?"

Our strongest belief—and we will state this outright—is that the experiences of the Last Third of life, whether we are hale or frail, gain meaning and even joy when we see them through the eyes of God. In Philippians 2:5 Paul tells us to "let the same mind be in you that was in Christ Jesus." This book represents our attempt to do just that—not only for you, our readers, but for ourselves as well. We all need to be reminded of God's love for us over and over and over.

We would like to acknowledge our appreciation to Robin Pippin, who has served for many years as our editor, advocate, adviser, and friend, and without whose constant support this book would never have come to fruition. We also express our appreciation to Rita Collett, our long-suffering editor, whose skill is seen in every paragraph, if not in every line.

Finally, we ask one thing of you: in reading and reflecting, examine your reactions to and interpretations of your later-life experiences so far, as well as noting your fears of the future. If your fears and interpretations rely on the secular—that is, seen through society's eyes—then try a different approach: "Put on the mind of Christ," and reexamine them. You may be amazed at the difference in the way you feel about the gift that is your life!

*W*ell, let's get on with the book before we all get too much older!

GATEWAY 1
Facing Aging and Dying

—⟋⟋⟋—

For to me, living is Christ and dying is gain.

—Philippians 1:21

JANE

Go on a Pilgrimage

Scripture

"Pharaoh said unto Jacob, How old art thou? And Jacob said unto Pharaoh, The days of the years of my pilgrimage are a hundred and thirty years: few and evil have the days of the years of my life been, and have not attained unto the days of the years of the life of my fathers in the days of their pilgrimage" (GEN. 47:8-9, KJV).

"Thy statutes have been my songs in the house of my pilgrimage" (Ps. 119:54, KJV).

$\mathcal{M}$ANY PEOPLE HAVE adopted the term *journey* as the metaphor for life in the later years. The *Shorter Oxford English Dictionary* (5th Edition, 2002) defines the word *journey* as "an act of going from one place to another or of traveling for a specified distance or period of time; a march, a ride, a drive, etc.; an excursion, or expedition." While these definitions validly describe life from a secular viewpoint, they seem to imply that living the later years is a linear process without goal, meaning, or intention. The term *pilgrimage* better describes the life course for the Christ-follower. Wikipedia defines *pilgrimage* as "a journey or search of great moral or spiritual significance. Typically, it is a journey to a shrine or other location of importance to a person's beliefs and faith. . . . A person who makes such a journey is called a pilgrim." More than the term *journey*, the words *pilgrim* and *pilgrimage* imply a life of meaningful intent and spiritual intensity, a far more vital way of looking at the experience of the Last Third of life.

In this book, we reenvision later life not as a random series of events to be endured and adapted to but as an intentional movement toward God. Not just a journey but a purposeful, sacred search for our Beloved. When viewed in that light, whatever and whomever we encounter each moment of each day becomes an encounter with the holy, an event that can transform us, a signpost that points the way, leading us to our ultimate leap into God's embrace at our death. So in the Last Third, death becomes our sacred destination, not a place to be feared. The gateways we discuss represent significant milestones on the path as well as portals through which we pass to proceed to the next stage of our pilgrimage.

How do we become pilgrims? How do we understand living in our Last Third as the most important pilgrimage of our lives? The decision to go on a pilgrimage is uniquely our own. If we reenvision aging as a pilgrimage and ourselves as pilgrims, (1) we choose to realize that we no longer have to maintain the illusion that we are young. We don't even need to use the qualifying euphemism "young at heart." We discover that actions and behaviors once appropriate for our thirties, forties, and fifties no longer serve us well in our sixties, seventies, eighties, and ninety-plus. In fact, what served us usefully earlier may actually impede our growth in later life. (2) We acknowledge the limited nature of time; every moment brings an opportunity to experience God more fully. (3) We choose to believe that we are not only aging but we are following a call to advance—to go forth from the known and the comfortable into the unknown and often uncomfortable, perhaps even painful. (4) We choose not to retire from life but to refire into new life. (5) We choose to interpret all the physical, intellectual, emotional, social, and spiritual changes as new territory to traverse in our advancement. (6) We choose to see this aging process as our final pilgrimage—the one that will ultimately lead us to our Beloved, our Source. (7) We willingly and eagerly invite others to come with us and to help them along, just as we allow them to help us reach our sacred destination of heaven.

Reflection

- What have been your metaphors for aging?
- Have you ever been on a pilgrimage? What was that experience like? If not, do you know persons who have gone on pilgrimage? Consider asking them to relate their stories.
- How do you resonate with the interpretation of the Last Third as a pilgrimage?
- In what ways do you envision yourself as a pilgrim?
- Looking back, what allows you to reinterpret your aging experience as a pilgrimage?

JANE

Looking Age Straight in the Face

Scripture

"Who knows? Perhaps you have come to royal dignity for just such a time as this" (ESTHER 4:14).

*H*OW CAN WE LIVE our later years with "royal dignity" when we face a future of negative events in every area of life? Newly retired Angela came to me for spiritual counseling, saying, "I look at myself in the mirror, catch a fleeting glimpse of myself in a store window—and I hardly recognize the person looking back at me! *When did I get to look like a sixty-five-year-old woman?* Then I realize that I *am* sixty-five! In my mind's eye I am not that old. Inwardly, I seem to be stuck at twenty-two—the age when I began my life "for real"—as an independent adult, looking forward to the opportunities for growth and accomplishment! That "looking forward" attitude has served me well for the first two-thirds of my life. But I realize that it will not carry me through the rigors of the last third, when there's not much to look forward to except heaven! This is a difficult time for me. I realize that my future, my life from now until I die, will not be filled with accomplishments, leadership, recognition—all the things that make midlife so powerful! My health may fail and confine me to my home—or worse! Help! I feel like I'm falling off a cliff!"

I must admit that Angela's story evoked a great deal of anxiety in me, for I too am sixty-five and have experienced the same shock at suddenly seeing myself in a stray mirror in public. I look much better at home in my bathroom mirror, where I can tighten my facial muscles by smiling, adjust my hair, and fill in the fine lines with makeup. Regardless of how many lectures I give on positive aging, my gerontological education did not prepare me for the shock of the actual experience of entering the third-third of life!

I often ask people how old they'd say they were if they didn't know their actual age. Most of the men claim to be "thirty-fiveish." Most of the women say "twenty-five to thirty." What accounts for the discrepancy between our actual age and the age we feel ourselves to be? Is this inner-age experience a denial of our aging process? Were we happiest, most hopeful, most productive at that younger age? Could it be our "resurrection" age? Perhaps we simply resist the notion of the "royal dignity" of deep maturity, where self-esteem no longer helps and when self-respect becomes a more useful goal.

What's the difference? We gain self-esteem through the pride we take in ourselves when we've successfully accomplished what society expects of us. Self-respect involves the inner peace we experience when we act according to our deepest values, our true self—even when our actions run counter to society's demands. We acknowledge our contribution to society and combine it with the satisfaction that we have been—most of the time—true to ourselves. The dignity of old age comes from remaining true to who we really are in the midst of the realities and challenges that face us. The task is finding out how to do this as life changes.

Reflection

- How old would you be if you had never been told your age?
- Throughout your life, what have been the sources of your self-esteem? What aspects of yourself and your life evoke feelings of self-respect? Do you see the difference?
- How can you enjoy the dignity of self-respect for the rest of your life, no matter what the future holds? How can you emerge into "royal dignity for just such a time as this"?

𝓩 JANE

120—Blessing or Curse?

Scripture

Then the LORD said, "My spirit shall not abide in mortals forever, for they are flesh; their days shall be one hundred twenty years" (GEN. 6:3).

𝓕OR THE PAST THIRTY YEARS I have begun every workshop and retreat on the topic of aging in this way: "There's an old Jewish birthday blessing that states, 'May you live to be 120!' If someone said this to you on your next birthday, would you consider these words a birthday blessing or a curse?" Most of the participants usually reply, "It depends." Then I explore "depends" by asking what the blessings of such a long life might be and how the years could be a curse.

I don't ask the question jokingly, for in the past twenty years or so scientists have found that the maximum natural human life span is approximately 120 years; some researchers believe it is even longer than that. For the first time in the history of humankind we (or our children and grandchildren) may have the opportunity to live that long. In the past century we have added years to our lives at an unprecedented rate. Some anthropologists say that in Imperial Rome the average life span was about twenty-two years. A person born in 1900 had an average life span of forty-seven years. Today the average life span is about eighty.

In the course of nineteen centuries only twenty-five years were added to the number of years people could expect to live, but since 1900 we have added thirty-three! Is this good or bad news? At this moment in time, extreme longevity seems to be a two-edged sword: blessing and curse for the individual and for society. It's a blessing for those still in reasonably good mental and physical health, who have the skills and opportunity to enable them to make new relationships and to have a purpose in life, for those who have something to look forward to each day. We all wish for these things. But long life can be and often is a curse for those who become frail or limited in body and mind, to the extent that they can no longer control their lives. It's a curse for those who suffer from unmitigated pain; for those whose loved ones die and who lack the resources to create new and deep relationships; and for those who find themselves without a purpose in life, a reason for being, a sense of being needed. If 120 years is the biological life span, we will have to confront the realities of the blessings and curses—at least until a future time when the problems of debilitating diseases of mind and body and financial poverty are solved or lessened. If we don't, I fear that suicide may become increasingly common and accepted—perhaps encouraged.

Although I can see the secular logic of suicide or physician-assisted death as an option for dealing with the curses of later life, I have great reservation about this option. We need to keep in mind that the last life-lesson we teach our children before our death is *how* to die. As Christians, we teach them how to die well as followers of Christ. Suicide does not seem to be the appropriate model. Perhaps we need to ask ourselves, "What would an old, frail, ill Jesus do?"

Reflection

- Do you want to live to be 120? What would be good about it—how could it be a blessing to you? What are the negatives—how could it be a curse? What is your worst-case scenario?

- If you are living longer than you expected and your life does not measure up to your liking, does your relationship with God comfort you when fears invade your mind and soul?
- Does being a Christian enable you to find meaning and purpose and joy even if you have no control over your daily life?
- If you have answered no to the above questions, what would help you experience Jesus as good news until the day you die? What do you think an old, frail Jesus would do?

Richard

Affirm Your Age

Scripture

You shall rise before the aged, and defer to the old; and you shall fear your God: I am the LORD (LEV. 19:32).

WE LIVE IN A CULTURE that exalts youth and attempts to disguise age. A growing practice called antiaging medicine includes aesthetic surgery, restorative dentistry, and cosmetic dermatology. Face creams, face-lifts, and antiaging jeans that lift all the right places tout their ability to halt the march of aging. Billboards, television, Internet ads, and the persuasive ads in magazines all tend to focus on the worth of youth and the worthlessness of age. We are not far from what Shakespeare wrote, "Age, I do abhor thee; youth, I do adore thee."

While we applaud the marvels of modern medicine that make aging easier, no one can deny the inevitable losses and debilities that will come. Aging, like a giant vacuum cleaner, eventually sucks us up. Lotion and potions can smooth out wrinkles; dye can color the hair. But you cannot cover up the problems of getting old. Aging gives us more time to wear out more parts. Some believe that the Last Third of life offers only decline, disease, despair, and death—or being warehoused in a nursing home.

On the other hand, a media blitz touts the "new old age," which describes aging as a time of endless joy and fulfillment. For many of those who grow older and experience frailties and disabilities, it means putting on a happy face when bones may ache, minds fail, and hearts break with loss after loss. Our society's obsession with youth drives the creation of the myth of the "new old age."

The new way of valuing older people highlights their youthfulness and praises them for looking young.

Yet the Bible honors old age. The Bible commands us to rise in the presence of the aged and to show respect for the elderly. The writer of Proverbs states, "The glory of youths is their strength, but the beauty of the aged is their gray hair" (Prov. 20:29). Job asks, "Is wisdom with the aged and understanding in length of days?" (Job 12:12). We need to affirm our old age rather than deny it; welcome it, not resist it.

I can honestly say that I had the best time of my life between the ages of sixty-two and eighty-two. I did not experience the years after retirement as a time of withdrawal from the world. Nor did I feel shelved by a society obsessed with youth. On the contrary, those years provided new adventures and challenges I never would have dreamed of. Being older came as gift, a joy and a blessing far exceeding my younger years. And this is not to deny the realities of frailty and disability that I have suffered.

More of us are entering the Last Third of our life now than at any other time in history. As life expectancy continues to rise, more of us will find ourselves living much longer than did our parents and grandparents. These extra years, even decades, extend the blessings of life. May we affirm our glorious age and live out the Last Third of life with courage and joy.

Reflection

- How do you feel about aging? What do you look forward to and what do you fear?
- Granted reasonable health, what kind of person will you be in the Last Third of life, and what are your hopes and dreams for this new stage of life?

RICHARD

Long Life Is Not Enough

Scripture

Length of days is not what makes age honourable, nor
number of years the true measure of life; understanding, this
is grey hairs, untarnished life, this is ripe old age (Wisdom of
Solomon 4:8-9, NJB).

*B*IBLE WRITERS CONSIDERED long life a blessing. Ancient
Israelites were commanded to follow God's ways that they might
live a long life in the Promised Land (Deut. 5:33). God's gift is a
long life: "With long life I will satisfy them, and show them my
salvation" (Ps. 91:16). Medical science has given us these bonus
years. Most of us will outlive our parents and grandparents. By
2030, when the oldest baby boomers reach the age of eighty-five
and the youngest sixty-five, nearly 72 million people aged sixty-
five and older will live in the United States, an increase of more
than 100 percent since 2000. In the retirement community where
I live, the number of people ninety and older grows daily, and
some will become centenarians.

We follow medical counsel on how to live a long life and
practice good habits in diet and exercise that lead to wellness. A
supplement called resveratrol found in grapes, red wine, green
tea, and dark chocolate seems to activate antiaging genes. But in
our preoccupation with living longer, we may forget about living
fully. The writer of the Wisdom of Solomon understood that the
good life entails more than living *longer*. Only living well brings
understanding to old age and leads to an untarnished life. In *The
Imitation of Christ*, Thomas à Kempis wrote, "It is vanity to desire

to live long, and not to care to live well. It is vanity to mind only this present life, and not to make provision for those things which are to come."[1]

The Last Third of life presents us with the opportunity to develop increased depth, integrity, and character. If we choose to grow and develop true wisdom, we must be willing to do the necessary inner work as detailed in the seven gateways to spiritual growth. In the Last Third of life we cannot expect to put our lives on automatic pilot and glide into the Promised Land.

Two older people come to mind who wed a long life with growth in grace. Josie is one hundred and two years old. Despite being legally blind, she captivates those of us at the retirement center with her sparkling presence and contagious love of life. She remains active, enters into community life, and even plays poker with the help of friends. For a while she volunteered to listen to persons with dementia. Hers is the inner beauty of the soul.

A second older adult, John, had retired. Born into a poor African American family in the rural South, John knew the endless struggles of minority people. He overcame cancer and after retirement spent his later years managing a clothes closet at the Yokefellow Christian Center in the community. Countless numbers of poor and needy have found in John a person who not only clothes their bodies but also warms their souls. Josie and John model lives that go beyond the duration of their years through their donation to the community. They achieved what Erik Erikson called integrity as they could look back at their lives with no regret, only satisfaction. They exemplify what the Yoruba tribe in Africa calls "wisdom people."

Reflection

- Do you want to live to be one hundred years of age? Why or why not?

- In your mind's eye, make a composite of helpful older adult role models. Name the persons and list the qualities and attitudes that make them your mentors.
- Which of your hopes and dreams for your later years go beyond a long life?

[1]Thomas à Kempis, *The Imitation of Christ*, ed. Paul Simpson McElroy (Mount Vernon, NY: Peter Pauper Press, 1965), 8.

RICHARD

Still Flourishing in Old Age

Scripture

The righteous will flourish like a palm tree,
    they will grow like a cedar of Lebanon;
planted in the house of the LORD;
    they will flourish in the courts of our God.
They will still bear fruit in old age,
    they will stay fresh and green (Ps. 92:12-14, NIV).

SOME PEOPLE BELIEVE THAT LIFE peaks at some point and has an upward and downward slope on either side. The peak for some people comes in midlife and from that moment on, their life goes downhill. However, the psalmist contends that people will flourish and maintain vitality in old age: "they will still bear fruit." Growing older offers new adventures and opportunities that can transform our lives.

Life has its peaks and valleys in any age. Far too many people develop tunnel vision about growing older. They envision the later years as dealing with health issues and letting go of physical life. They miss the truth that this stage can open onto a broader and wider world where the soul finds its fullness. Even in old age, life can be lived full of genuine joy and new discoveries. Martin Buber wrote the following: "To be old is a glorious thing when one has not unlearned what it means to begin."[1]

Abram and Sarai serve as role models of old people who flourish in their later years. At age seventy-five Abram and Sarai leave all that is familiar—their country and people—to find a new home in the Last Third of their lives. They experience not only dislocation from home, a change of name and identity but also an unexpected pregnancy. Their first child, Isaac (whose name means "he laughs"), symbolizes the joyful rebirth possible in later life. Both Abram and Sarai became God's blessings and died at a good old age.

Nine years ago my wife and I made a similar journey of faith, leaving our home and, in a real sense, our identities, to begin a new life in a retirement community five hundred miles away. That journey continues in this new community as we try to serve and bless older residents. Our vitality, productivity, and service to others will not end as long as we live. We flourish and grow every day in the life of this community and give thanks that God has saved the best until last.

A tourist, tramping about in the villages of New England, came upon an old woman sitting in silence on the front porch of her cabin. The tourist asked, "Lived here all your life?" She replied, "Not yet." That is the spirit of the older person who lives every day with joy and expectation.

Reflection

- If you are retired, consider the interests you have put aside over the years, saying, "When I have enough time I will do this." Write them down, and review your list. Are there any whose time has come?
- A successful bank CEO tells you that since retirement he feels he has gone from "who's who" to "who's he?" What would you suggest to help him flourish in retirement?
- If Martin Buber correctly notes that being old can be glorious when you have not unlearned how to begin again, write down some new ventures for your later years.

[1]Martin Buber, *Meetings: Autobiographical Fragments*, 3rd ed. (New York, Routledge, 2002), 59.

RICHARD

Practice Dying

Scripture

For all our days pass away under your wrath;
  our years come to an end like a sigh.

. . . .

So teach us to count our days
  that we may gain a wise heart (Ps. 90:9, 12).

*B*EHIND THE ALTAR ON THE EAST WING of the chapel of
a Trappist monastery high up in the Rocky Mountains hangs a
simple wooden cross. It remains there until it is taken down to
mark the grave of the next brother to die. Whenever the monks
face the altar, they also face the simple and immediate symbol of
their own death.

Death can serve as our wake-up call, reminding us that our
days have a finite number, that the sands in the hourglass slowly
slip away. Socrates advised his pupils to practice for dying and
death. He knew that facing death made life more precious, and
every day remains a gift. Still many people, even in their last years,
deny death by shoving it under the table. Many people choose
to fill their traveling years with conversation about the scenery
rather than the final destination. Others of us deny and dread
death because we fear the pain of death and the loss of ourselves.

Living in a community where the angel of death often visits, I cannot escape thoughts of death. The community memorial
board hangs a few feet from my apartment. Every time I pass that
board I cannot help but wonder, *When will my name appear?* I
attend many funerals; I stand at many gravesides. One wintry day

as the tent poles clanked in the wind, I reflected on the time when everyone would return from the cemetery except me.

The psalmist contrasts God's eternity with humanity's transience. The psalm tells us to "count our days that we may gain a wise heart." Keeping death at arm's length can prevent us from embracing our lives. For this reason, the rule of Saint Benedict makes the following assertion: "Day by day remind yourself that you are going to die."[1] Rather than reflecting a morbid obsession with death, awareness of our mortality helps us focus our minds and hearts on the essentials. It can sharpen our sense of what is important as we realize that any moment could be our last. So we choose to invest our energy and time in matters of significance.

"Is there life after death," a disciple once asked a Holy One. And the Holy One answered, "The great spiritual question is not 'Is there life after death' but 'Is there life before death?'" Practice dying. Life and death form one process. Paul said it well, "If we live, we live to the Lord, and if we die, we die to the Lord; so then, whether we live or whether we die, we are the Lord's" (Rom. 14:8).

Reflection

- As you grow older, do you find yourself thinking more or less about your death? Explain.
- Can you envision a "happy" death? If so, what would that look like?
- Write out your wishes for your death, answering questions like these: Where do you want to be when you die? Whom do you want with you when you die? What would be your music preference as you die?
- Describe other wishes. You might want to include these wishes with your living will and memorial or funeral plans.

[1]Timothy Fry and others, eds., *The Rule of St. Benedict in English* (New York: Vintage Books, 1998), 13.

GATEWAY 2
Living with Limitations

———◦◦◦———

"My grace is sufficient for you,
for power is made perfect in weakness."
So I will boast all the more gladly of my weaknesses,
so that the power of Christ may dwell in me.

—2 CORINTHIANS 12:9

Richard

Limited But Renewed

Scripture

So we do not lose heart. Even though our outer nature is wasting away, our inner nature is being renewed day by day (2 Cor. 4:16).

OLDER PERSONS WILL SUFFER from chronic illnesses and health problems that last for an extended period of time, and most have no cure. Science may develop drugs to alleviate some of the worst health problems of the old, but the drugs will not be available for us today. Furthermore, as I live out my last years in a retirement community, I am all the more convinced that people who live beyond their eighties can expect extended medical issues before they die.

When I was in my late sixties, I led a conference on aging. An older man approached me after my session and said, "What do you know about aging? Wait until you're my age." He was eighty three. He was right! As I live in my eighty-third year, I know some of these limitations all too well. It is easy to know the literature of aging; it's quite another thing to live it.

Spinal stenosis has slowed me down, and I rely on a cane to walk without falling. Sometimes I creak to my feet, bending forward to keep my balance. Ataxic gait has caused balance and walking problems, and at times I find myself needing help to avoid falling. Little things have become big things, and it takes more effort to do the simplest things. I had to accept the reality of these limitations and have had to alter my lifestyle. Yet, I have no complaints, for every day is a gift.

Paul talks about two kinds of personal existence. The "outer" person that wastes away represents our whole self, subject to the limits and diminishment of aging. Human existence falls prey to the power of suffering and decay. But Paul adds, "our inner nature is being renewed day by day." This spiritual renewal takes place daily in the person united to Christ. This inner life of the Spirit will be known fully in the age to come.

I believe that the hype about older people undertaking youthful endeavors like cross-country skiing and wakeboarding neglects the youthful spirit of the older person whose physical constraints require the use of a walker, wheelchair, or scooter.

Osteoporosis has wrecked Marie Shepherd's body. Multiple fractures of wrists and legs restrict her to a wheelchair. Despite numerous bouts in skilled nursing for rehabilitation, Marie returns to our community and maintains her cheerful spirit. Her disability has attuned her to the suffering of others, fostering a deep compassion. Despite her pain she exemplifies what Kathleen Fischer calls "winter grace": "courage grown larger in the face of diminishment."[1]

Reflection

- If you are an older person, what are some of the limits old age has placed upon you? How do you deal with them?
- Whom do you know whose lives reflect compassion and concern for others despite their limitations?
- What is your response to the prayer, "May you die young at a very old age?"

[1]Kathleen Fischer, *Winter Grace: Spirituality and Aging* (Nashville, TN: Upper Room Books, 1998), 12.

RICHARD

Don't Get Around Much Anymore

Scripture

For I am ready to fall,
> and my pain is ever with me.

. . . .

Do not forsake me, O LORD;
O my God, do not be far from me;
> make haste to help me,
O Lord, my salvation (Ps. 38:17, 21).

*T*HREE YEARS AGO I WENT to the hospital for one problem, only to discover another. My doctor diagnosed me with lumbar spinal stenosis, a narrowing of space in the spine that puts pressure on the spine. Stenosis can result in clumsiness, frequent pain, and heaviness in the legs. Since that diagnosis I have done weeks of physical therapy and continued a disciplined regimen of exercise. I now walk with a cane and manage with a minimum of pain.

I cannot live in the same manner as I did before this malady affected me. I have learned to live with this problem and have been spared extreme pain, but I know the lack of mobility will be with me forever. At times I feel I am living on the edge, always fearful of falling. Many of our residents have had serious falls that led to broken bones, often a precursor of permanent residence in skilled nursing.

The nagging presence of this disability has slowed me down, and I don't get around as much as I used to. I restrict my driving to brief daytime trips to the drugstore or post office. My visits to grandchildren scattered across the country from California to

Texas have about ended. So in some ways my life parallels my spinal problem: it is narrowed down to a small space in this retirement community.

My life had been restricted by serious complications from surgery in 1992, but I recovered and thus ended that suffering. My current situation is different. This lack of mobility will be with me until I leave this earth. At times my body feels like an old car, repainted and refurbished, able to make a few trips but no longer reliable for the long journeys.

When my wife and I moved to this community nine years ago, I noted one walker and two scooters. Now, forty-one people use walkers, and eight people use scooters. Yet I see blessings in this problem of aging. It has given me precious time for God, a time for contemplation and listening to what God would say to me in this "unformed time." It has helped me feel more compassion for the people with whom I live. For them and myself, I pray with the psalmist, "Do not forsake me, O Lord; O my God, do not be far from me." God has answered my prayers with a strong presence that will never forsake them or me.

Reflection

- If growing older gives you more time for the contemplative life, write down several ideas or words you associate with the aging process.
- What relationship do you see between the contemplative life and the active life of doing? Do the two approaches seem opposed, in competition, complementary? Explain.

Richard

Aging's Double Whammy

Scripture

Remember your creator in the days of your youth, before the days of trouble come, . . . before the sun and the light and the moon and the stars are darkened and the clouds return with the rain (Eccl. 12:1–2).

$\mathcal{M}$ANY YEARS AGO I ATTENDED a conference on aging. In several sessions, the leaders chose to simulate some physical limitations of aging. I received thick plastic glasses smeared with petroleum jelly so I could hardly see. Then a nurse stuffed thick earplugs in my ears so I could scarcely hear anything. Then a cotton ball was stuffed in my nostrils so I could hardly breathe. At this point, I had a real grasp of those problems. Hearing loss and dimmed vision are the double whammy of aging that many older persons face.

The writer of Ecclesiastes seemingly knew full well what it meant for older people to experience so many limitations. His words still ring true for those of us who are old.

The Mayo Clinic in Minnesota claims that one-third of older persons suffer from hearing loss. Just eating a meal in my retirement community helps persons realize that most older folks suffer from hearing loss. Some older adults with hearing loss withdraw because they feel left out, while others become overly talkative to cover up the lack of hearing. Some wear hearing aids, but one man told me he turned his off when he came to the dining room. He simply smiles and nods his head, because "no one says anything worth hearing." I have some hearing loss. When I went to an audiologist who told me that hearing aids would cost five thousand dollars, I replied, "What did you say?"

Most older people suffer from vision loss. I had cataract removals on both eyes and later a laser treatment. Finally, my ophthalmologist said, "There's nothing more I can do for you." When I looked at the computer screen, it was a blur. I felt doomed to fading vision. Older people often discuss which of the two losses they fear the most: deafness or blindness. I fear losing my vision. I felt my writing days were history and a significant part of me had come to an end. My optician became a real-life good Samaritan. He suggested that I get computer glasses, and I was amazed when I could see the screen and write this book.

My friend Jesse, who is blind, reminded me that although he had lost his sight, he had never lost his vision! The limitations of old age became gateways to spiritual growth. With outer light and perfect sight we only see the surface of things. But if we see by the inner light within us and listen to God, we experience a new sense of God's presence.

Reflection

- If you had to choose between the loss of sight and the loss of vision, which would you choose? Why?
- How can an older person with fading vision and hearing loss compensate for these losses?

RICHARD

Downsized But Growing

Scripture

[Jesus] said to them, "Take care! Be on your guard against all kinds of greed; for one's life does not consist in the abundance of possessions" (Luke 12:15).

$\mathcal{A}$ MAJOR ISSUE my wife and I faced when moving to a retirement community was smaller living space. We had to rid ourselves of possessions in order to fit. Psychologists claim that anxiety comes in two forms: expanded and compacted. Expanded anxiety comes with heightened sensitivity to stimuli, both from within and without. Compacted anxiety occurs when a person lives in a small space and feels boxed in and confined. I find myself content in living in a smaller space, but I still miss the spaciousness of our former home.

However, clearing out the clutter, downsizing possessions to live in a smaller space, has been a cleansing experience. It has also helped my wife and me evaluate all we have come to know about life. We now look for meaning above the things of the world for the sake of what is yet to come. In this Last Third of life we can travel light, paring down to essential possessions. The patriarch Job knew full well that "naked I came from my mother's womb, and naked shall I return there" (Job 1:21).

The Hasidim tell the story of the American tourist who visited the renowned rabbi Hofetz Chaim. The emptiness and barrenness of the rabbi's one-room house shocked the visitor. The simple room contained books, a table, and a bench. "Rabbi," asked the tourist, "where is your furniture?" The rabbi asked, "Where is yours?" "Mine?" asked the puzzled American. "I'm only passing through. "So am I," the rabbi replied.

Abbot Christopher Jamison relates that English Benedictine monks annually during Lent have the custom of writing out what they call a "poverty bill." They record an inventory of everything they have for personal use and hand the list to the abbot. What they don't need, they give away. Such a practice offers a creative approach to realizing what they can do without, as well as giving some of their possessions away.

When my wife and I entered this retirement community, we stripped down the possessions we had accrued through the years. I gave my car to my grandson and gave most of my library to clergy and the church. As we continue to downsize our possessions and simplify life, we bear witness to a radical detachment from worldly things and defy the cultural gospel of prosperity. We have learned that life is more than things; the self is larger than what we possess of material goods. We refuse to believe that what we have is what we are. In the Last Third of life, what matters is the shaping of the soul that allows us to be who God intends us to be. Often the words of an old hymn come to mind:

> I thank Thee, Lord, that Thou hast kept the best in store;
> We have enough, yet not too much to long for more:
> A yearning for a deeper peace not known before.
> —Adelaide Anne Procter, "My God, I Thank Thee"

Reflection

- If you live in a retirement community and had to leave your home and downsize your possessions, what was that like for you?
- If you are living at home, what can you do without? What can you give away? What would you list in your poverty bill?

Richard

Bent But Not Broken

Scripture

Now [Jesus] was teaching in one of the synagogues on the sabbath and just then there appeared a woman with a spirit that had crippled her for eighteen years. She was bent over and was quite unable to stand up straight (Luke 13:10-11).

Some time ago I gave a presentation at a retirement community. The program ended, and residents left for their apartments. I noticed one older couple slowly making their way down the walk. She was bent over, suffering from arthritis or osteoporosis; he seemed extremely frail, leaning on her as they walked into the night. In their frailty they represent a growing number of older people in our culture.

The story of the bent-over woman is tucked away in Luke's Gospel and often ignored. Although the Gospel does not indicate her age, her plight affects many older women. We know that she had suffered eighteen years from the wear and tear of her crippling disease. The woman, bent over at the waist, had to view life from the level of half her stature. Medical science today might say she suffered from spondylosis, where the bones in her back fused together in a rigid mass. The disease is a chronic progressive form of arthritis. What might have begun with lower back pain has ended in a horrible, painful condition.

Bent over, the woman could not see the sun or moon, only the ground. No doubt many people looked away when her sideways glance met their stares. Yet she came to the synagogue on the sabbath day. Her priorities were a lot straighter than those of many who walk erect. She had not come for healing; she wished to worship. Her gift came in her availability to God's grace. Then Jesus found her. Moved with compassion, he called her forward and told her, "Woman, you are set free from your ailment." Jesus healed her, and she walked away standing upright.

Many older people suffer from infirmities of the spine. Some are bent over like the woman in the Gospel story. They use a walker to get where they need to go. Others have arthritis that results in back pain. I rarely hear such folks complain about their limitations. They zoom up and down the halls of this community on their walkers and scooters. Their bodies are bent over, but their spirits are not broken.

A woman once visited the studio of the great artist, Michelangelo. It grieved her to see him hacking away at the beautiful marble. She argued with the sculptor about the loss as she pointed to the chips that littered the floor. "What a waste," she said. Michelangelo replied, "The more the marble wastes, the more the statue grows." Like the bent-over woman in the Gospel story, the years can hack away at our bodies. But living with courage helps a person grow in grace. Like Paul, who never was delivered from the thorn in his flesh, "power is made perfect in weakness."

Reflection

- Repeat this prayer until it becomes part of you.

  When your youthful days are done,
  and old age is stealing on,
  and your body bends beneath the weight of care,
  [God] will never leave you then,
  [God] will go with you to the end,
  take your burden to the Lord
  and leave it there.
  —Charles A. Tindley, "Leave It There"

JANE

Jesus' Promise

Scripture

Jesus said to Peter, "Very truly, I tell you, when you were younger, you used to fasten your own belt and to go wherever you wished. But when you grow old, you will stretch out your hands, and someone else will fasten a belt around you and take you where you do not wish to go." (He said this to indicate the kind of death by which [Peter] would glorify God.) After this he said to him, "Follow me" (John 21:17-19).

*T*HIS PASSAGE SOUNDS AS THOUGH Jesus is predicting life in a nursing home or time spent in a rehab center for Peter's old age, doesn't it? It's a situation many people find themselves in and others fear experiencing in their future.

What is the origin of the fear? We don't want to lose any control over our bodies, minds, and the plans we have for our lives. Also, we despise the idea of being a burden to other people. Unfortunately, we live in a society where each person is expected to "carry his or her own weight." Fierce independence is a secular virtue. We respond well to immediate and time-limited needs, such as those incurred by flood or tornado victims; but we have little empathy and patience for those who need permanent help over the long haul (including ourselves).

The idea of being a burden—of not contributing to others and to society—weighs heavily on us, especially as we venture into frail or even ill elderhood. Some people in their fifties who care for parents with failing health fear that the same sense of burden and uselessness will happen to them. Many have told me of their plans to take their own lives before they are too incapacitated to do so. But how are we, in our faith tradition, to deal with physical and mental diminishment? Is hopelessness all we have to look forward to?

The above passage from John's Gospel offers a different way of viewing our losses—a positive, energizing, life-giving way. Often when we read this scripture, we pay attention to the image of Peter being constrained with a belt from going where he wants to go. We can just see his wife or daughter hanging on to the other end of the belt and scolding, "Papa, let the younger Christians do the preaching now! You've done your part; there's nothing more you can do—you're too old and infirm. Stay here and rest; you've earned it!" That image is pretty depressing. Few people pay attention to the next two sentences, "He said this to indicate the kind of death by which [Peter] *would glorify God*. After this he said to him, 'Follow me'" (emphasis added).

For me, this passage is one of the most encouraging of the entire New Testament, for Jesus promises his active, extroverted, energetic friend Peter—his chosen leader—that even when he can no longer do the work of preaching, teaching, and leading the Christian community, *he will still be able to glorify God*—using, in some mysterious way, the suffering of that condition. Only after Jesus assures Peter that he is empowered to do God's work in all life's circumstances does Jesus invite Peter to "follow me."

Many Christians, lay and ordained, who have worked hard for God and for the church experience distress when they retire or can no longer pastor, preach, teach, help, and do "official" good works. They often feel a sense of uselessness to the kingdom of God or that they are letting God down. This is not so, for Jesus reassures all of his followers that they will continue to "glorify God."

Reflection

- In what ways are you able and called to glorify God if or when you are bedridden, receiving total care from strangers, or living away from your beloved home and the people you love?

JANE

Why Doesn't God Take Me?

Scripture

Jesus said to [Peter], "Very truly, I tell you, when you were younger, you used to fasten your own belt and to go wherever you wished. But when you grow old, you will stretch out your hands, and someone else will fasten a belt around you and take you where you do not wish to go." (He said this to indicate the kind of death by which [Peter] would glorify God.) After this he said to him, "Follow me" (John 21:17-19).

1 GREATLY FEAR being so mentally and physically impaired that not only must I depend on strangers to care for me but I no longer have a "voice," a way to contribute to society through writing or speaking. Frail older adults often ask me why they have to go on living when they can no longer contribute to their community in the way they prefer or when they can no longer care for themselves. "Why doesn't God take me?" is a lament I hear all too often when people believe they have come to the point of being a burden rather than a blessing to their families or to society.

Being dependent, requiring someone else to "fasten a belt around" us also means that we are powerless in many ways. And powerlessness—loss of personal power—is one of the greatest sufferings of old age. From a secular perspective, hundreds of books have been written and workshops presented to help people become more powerful—physically, emotionally, socially, financially, occupationally—even spiritually! Because society greatly values power, we find relinquishing power extremely difficult when that becomes necessary.

In secular society, the question "Why doesn't God take me?" may be a reasonable question to ask, but Jesus teaches otherwise. One of the hardest lessons for a Christ-follower to learn is that secular power is not always the highest level of power.

In the above passage from John, Jesus has just commissioned Peter to take over as the primary promoter of Jesus' teaching—certainly a promotion to a position of power among the disciples! Put another way, Jesus has just handed over the keys of the kingdom to Peter, a heady experience for the fellow. Can you imagine how "puffed up" and empowered Peter must have felt? In his next breath, however, Jesus assures the impetuous Peter that someday his situation will change. When Peter grows old and can no longer care for himself, when others dress him and lead him around, taking him to places against his will, Peter will continue to glorify God—perhaps because of his situation of powerlessness.

The Gospel offers this hopeful gift to frail elders (and those who fear becoming frail). Jesus promises us that somehow, even though we may be bedridden, lying in a B-grade nursing home, we may—because of our frailty, not in spite of it—be a source of God's glorification. This may be one of the purest, least ego-filled ways in which we will have glorified God in our entire lives!

Reflection

- What kind of powerlessness do you fear the most?
- What kind of power have you lost because of your age?
- How do you act when you feel powerless?
- When have you used your powerlessness to help someone?
- How can you glorify God in the powerlessness you are experiencing now or fear the most in the future?

GATEWAY 3
Doing Inner Work

———⟨⟨∅⟩⟩———

I have been crucified with Christ; and it is no longer I who live,
but it is Christ who lives in me.

—GALATIANS 2:19-20

JANE

The Work of Forgiving

Scripture

"For if you forgive others their trespasses, your heavenly Father
will also forgive you; but if you do not forgive others, neither
will your Father forgive your trespasses" (Matt. 6:14-15).

*T*HERE ARE TWO SIDES to forgiveness. Some people refuse to forgive themselves and never let go of the guilt they feel (even if they
have been forgiven by whomever they offended). They make themselves miserable. On the other hand, many people harbor grudges
for years, withholding forgiveness from others, even close family
members. A friend recently told me that whenever he visits his
ninety-five-year-old mother, she spends the greater part of their
visit listing all the people she feels have "done her wrong." Most
of them are long dead, many of them church members! Even with
her failing memory, she can recall every detail of the offenses—
and relishes listing them over and over. Because her grudges are
the main topic of conversation, few people want to visit, and she
is experiencing increasing isolation. My own two aunts died after
sixty years of never having forgiven each other for some offense.
Over the course of those years their bitterness and refusal to talk
with each other split the family in two and denied their children
and grandchildren the opportunity to know one another.

In the Lord's Prayer, Jesus makes it clear that *our* forgiveness hinges on our willingness to forgive others. Forgiveness is
an important requirement for friendship with God and other
people, as well as for our own good health. The act of forgiving
undergirds our physical, emotional, social, and spiritual health.

Researchers in secular universities are attempting to determine the specific bodily effects that occur when a person forgives or refuses to forgive. So far, they have found that refusal to forgive has negative effects on physical health.

If forgiveness is so integral to our health, why do we hold so tightly to our anger, making ourselves increasingly miserable? One reason comes in our thinking that to forgive lets the offender off the hook. We want *our* version of justice—retribution; we want the offender to suffer in some way for what s/he has done. *Webster's Dictionary* says that to forgive is "to give up resentment or claim to requital [revenge] on account of an offense." To forgive completely we must willingly give up the wish that something bad will befall the offender. Then we allow the gnawing feeling of resentment toward him or her to die away (which it will over time, if we change our desire for revenge). We also tend to think that forgiveness requires reconciliation, which is not true. Reconciling, or getting back into relationship again, comes only after the act of forgiving and may or may not occur (and sometimes should not occur, depending on the offense). We can always forgive without reconciling. By forgiving we let ourselves off the hook of ongoing misery.

Reflection

- Is there anyone you are refusing to forgive? How is your inability to forgive affecting the quality of your life? How is it affecting your relationship with God?
- Who, now living, needs your forgiveness? Who, no longer living, needs your forgiveness?
- What are your barriers to forgiving them? What do you need to do to release them from your anger? If you don't know, is there someone you can ask for help?

JANE

Rummaging for God

Scripture

In Christ we have also obtained an inheritance, having been destined according to the purpose of him who accomplishes all things according to his counsel and will, so that we, who were the first to set our hope on Christ, might live for the praise of his glory (Eph. 1:11).

$\mathcal{R}$ON AND I GATHER with friends once a month for spiritual challenge and support, all of us sharing what we find helpful (or not) in our attempt to grow closer to God. One friend, retired pastor Wayne Anderson, told us of a practice he employs, which he calls "rummaging for God" in the events of the day. Each night as he lies in bed awaiting sleep, he sifts through the day's encounters with people, the glimpses of nature, the work he has done. He tries to discover where God has shone through, where the Spirit's action in events had gone unnoticed at the time. He says he usually finds so many that he falls asleep before he recalls them all!

I really appreciate this practice. I grew up with the traditional spiritual discipline called "examination of conscience." Each night I recalled the day's events to note where I slipped up, missed the mark, could have done a better job for God. This recounting always resulted in a sense of guilt. Granted, it was a humbling experience, but a negative one on which to end the day. Also, the practice emphasized *me*—what *I* did for God—rather than evoking gratitude for what God had done for me and others.

"Rummaging for God" seems particularly appropriate if we're on a pilgrimage into the Last Third of life. Looking for evidence of God's activity in our lives has the power to transform our attitude from disappointment with self to ever-growing gratitude toward

God, who is intimately involved with us. Many psychologists have found that two powerful characteristics of "successful aging" are these: (1) willingness to forgive and (2) a strong sense of gratitude. Wayne states that as he practices "rummaging for God" he experiences an ever-increasing awareness and ability to see God working in the "little things" of his life during the day—as they happen—rather than late at night before he sleeps.

With this awareness of God's activity will come a spirit of joyful anticipation and a sense of profound gratitude for all of life. Gratitude cannot help but flow into thankfulness and then into praise. Rummaging for God will emerge into a life lived to the praise of God's glory.

Reflection

- Do you practice anything like "rummaging for God"? If so, how does it affect the quality of your life?
- If you haven't attempted this practice on a regular basis, try it for one week. At the end of each day, write down how God has shone through in the ordinariness of your everyday life. As you examine your recordings at week's end, do you find that you are noticing more and more of God's gifts?
- What resistance might you have to rummaging for evidence of God in your daily life?

JANE

Envy: A Deadly Sin of Later Life

Scripture

But when [Joseph's] brothers saw that their father loved him more than all his brothers, they hated him, and could not speak peaceably to him (Gen. 37:4).

REMEMBER THE SEVEN deadly sins? Traditionally, they are wrath, greed, sloth, pride, lust, envy, and gluttony. They are called "deadly" sins because most of the other sins we commit originate from these. Over the years I've observed and personally experienced that the characteristics of the famous seven deadly sins—or their manifestations—often change with age. A case in point . . .

Helen, a one-hundred-year-old retired professor of nursing, had been my mother's best friend, outliving my mom by forty-six years. Helen became one of my lifelong mentors. She lived in a lovely apartment in Greenwich Village; whenever I had a chance to go to New York, I eagerly accepted her hospitality. We would stay up well past midnight playing Scrabble and catching up on each other's lives.

Until her death at 102, Helen was the only person alive who had known me since my birth; she was forty when I was born and had been like a member of the family for all of my life. Both registered nurses, she and my mother had met in the registration line at Columbia University Teachers College in 1929. Both had wanted to teach nursing and were enrolling in a BA degree program that would qualify them to do so. Helen went on to earn her PhD, ultimately completing her teaching career having been dean of schools of nursing at two prestigious universities.

After Helen's retirement at sixty-five—still full of enormous energy—she worked for the World Health Organization, developing hospitals in rural areas of countries in the Middle East. When she retired from the WHO, she recorded books for the sight-impaired and taught reading to adults. Needless to say, Helen exemplified optimal, successful aging! When she died, she had never had a sick day in her life! Nor did she experience the pain of arthritis or any other chronic ailment. As a New Yorker she didn't own a car, so she walked everywhere. She could have been the poster child for the kind of life we are trying to live into in old age! Sounds like an idyllic life, doesn't it? She was my hero for as long as I can remember. I wanted to be just like her when I grew up.

One evening when Helen was in her midnineties and we were playing a highly competitive game of Scrabble (she always won), Helen told me about a dark cloud in her blue sky. Her dear friend Emma, age eighty-five, had recently ended their friendship. There had been no disagreement and no change in interests. Emma gave only one reason for ending the relationship: Helen's perfect health, mobility, with no aches or pains while Emma, ten years younger, was riddled with pain and joint damage from rheumatoid arthritis that caused her to be wheelchair-bound and dependent on others. Emma frankly admitted to Helen that she envied her health and that she couldn't tolerate being around Helen because her vital presence reminded Emma of her own pain and dependency. Emma's envy created such pain that she decided to end the relationship. She told Helen she no longer wanted Helen to visit her in the assisted living apartment. Emma totally shut Helen out of her life. They never saw each other or talked on the telephone again. That blow to their friendship devastated Helen.

At the time of this sharing I was in my midfifties and couldn't fathom Emma's envy. Her behavior lay beyond my experience and comprehension. I was very critical of her; Helen, however, seemed to understand, her response being sadness rather than anger.

The story differs now that I am in my midsixties and have experienced cancer, congestive heart failure, neuropathy of fingers and toes, and impaired eyesight due to a macular hole in my retina. Now I can understand Emma's situation perfectly. I find myself observing friends and others in their seventies, eighties, and nineties who have more energy than I ever thought of having. They are healthy, active, and doing wonderful work—both paid and volunteer! I have to admit to experiencing the deadly sin of envy because I realize the likelihood that I will probably not grow old in the same vigorous way. I had always thought I would be one of those exemplar older adults—now I have to do the inner work of coming to terms with envy that could easily prevent me from relishing the gifts I have been given for the joy of my unique life. I keep reminding myself of advice given to me by a patient newly diagnosed with Alzheimer's disease. When I asked her why she seemed so undisturbed by the diagnosis she said, "Honey, I don't worry about what I don't have, or I'd never be happy!"

Reflection

- Most of us have been besieged by envy at some time during our lives. Have you experienced any situation like that of Emma? Helen?
- How has aging changed your experience of envy?
- What makes you envious of others? Which of your gifts could be a source of envy for others?
- Do you tend to focus on what you do not have instead of the gifts you do have?

JANE

Pride: Another Deadly Sin

Scripture

"For all who exalt themselves will be humbled, and those who humble themselves will be exalted" (Luke 14:11).

*A*REN'T WE SUPPOSED TO BE proud of ourselves and of those we love? When does pride become more than deserved self-respect or respect for our own? When does it cross the line to become a deadly sin? And how does the deadly sin of pride rear its ugly head in later life? In earlier life, pride manifests as an attitude of smugness coupled with arrogant behavior toward others. We most often associate pride with winning, being number one, unique achievement. We don't recognize the danger in competitive spirit, but it is quite evident at the end of major ball games when the winning team's supporters "celebrate" to the point of harming property and injuring lives.

With pride's close association with competition in earlier life, how does it manifest itself in later years? Often a certain subtle smugness when comparing ourselves with others who are not aging as successfully as we are can occur. Recently I overheard three men talking about their medications. Two of them needed significant numbers of meds to keep themselves alive and were reluctantly resigned to their plight. The third—the same age—needed no medications. I could hear the smug satisfaction and the judgmental attitude in his voice when he boasted to the others, "I've never had to take any meds—it comes from doing all the right things. You know, exercise, healthy diet. If you guys had watched your weight instead of all those games on TV. . . . " I watched the vitality of the two men disappear as their "friend" made them aware of their inadequacies. (This conversation could easily have led them to the sin of envy—or even despair.)

Most often, however, I think the competition turns inward. I compete with my younger self, which manifests in the refusal to acknowledge the signs of age. I cling to a prideful vision of myself at a favorite younger age. (Mine is twenty-seven!)

Here are some examples. When I was younger my hearing was excellent—there's nothing wrong with it now! (Yet I get annoyed at my spouse's mumbling and refuse to have my hearing tested.) When I was younger my eyesight was so good I didn't even need glasses. I wear them now and they work just fine. I'll bet I have 20/20 vision. (Yet I've had four bumper-thumpers in the last year because I didn't see the car behind me in the parking lot.) When I was forty I ran ten miles a day and competed in two Boston Marathons! (Don't tell me I need to use a cane or a walker. What are a few falls? I haven't broken anything!) I am perfectly capable of living here in my own house—I don't *ever* want to hear talk about assisted living again! (Yet, I get angry when you don't bring me my groceries on time or clean my house the way I want it done.)

Reflection

- How often have you resisted help because it implies that you are getting older?
- If someone told you that you looked at least fifteen years younger than your chronological age, would you consider that a compliment or an insult?
- Do you ever lie about your age?
- Do you find yourself spending time with older people so that you can take pride in being the youngest, most vivacious one?

Richard

Afternoon Work

Scripture

Work out your own salvation with fear and trembling; for it is God who is at work in you, enabling you both to will and to work for his good pleasure (Phil. 2:12).

CARL JUNG WROTE, "A human being would certainly not grow to be seventy or eighty years old if this longevity had no meaning for the species to which he belongs. The afternoon of human life must also have a significance of its own and cannot be merely a pitiful appendage to life's morning."[1] The later years provide a rich opportunity to work on ourselves and be who we are. The first half of life is one-sided, busy with career and family. We have little time to cultivate our inner lives.

Paul urges us to *work out* our salvation, not *work for* our salvation. God in Christ has taken care of our ultimate salvation. Unlike Atlas, we do not have to carry the weight of our sins on our backs. We are saved by grace and not by works. But being conformed to the image of Christ takes effort; in our later years we can grow as we work on ourselves.

We may find ourselves subtly tempted to stay in our comfort zones or habitual routines rather than grow or explore new experiences. Once an automobile heads toward its destination (guided by GPS), cruise control can be activated. When the desired speed is achieved, the driver can sit back and relax. Not so with the later years if we are to grow in grace.

Denying our egos, being more attentive to others' needs takes hard work. A prevalent myth states that older persons cannot change. We can change, but it takes hard work. It will not happen overnight; giving up *our* needs and demands and living to serve others is a daily discipline.

We see a classic example of afternoon work in the later years of the Russian novelist Leo Tolstoy. He felt uncomfortable with the wide acclaim his writing had brought him. A growing emptiness inside haunted him; he felt lost and disconnected from his soul. In his spiritual testament, *A Confession*, he wrote, "My life came to a standstill. . . . There was no life."[2] In his later years he began to live a life of simplicity and service patterned after Christ's teaching in the Sermon on the Mount.

As we work on ourselves, a new aspect of ourselves begins to unfold, and we come in touch with a newness of life. When we work out our own salvation, God is at work in us. We may be unaware of this work in us, but God is there, giving us strength and grace to grow. As we grow in Christlikeness, we receive assurance of God's promise, "The one who began a good work among you will bring it to completion by the day of Jesus Christ" (Phil. 1:6).

Reflection

- Spend some time in quiet meditation. Clear your mind of all distractions:
  Visualize your earlier years as a parent and career person or both. Pause a few minutes. Then visualize your current life. Notice the difference. How can you use this radical freedom, this extended time, to become your true self apart from roles?

[1]Carl Gustav Jung, *Modern Man in Search of a Soul*, trans. W. S. Dell and Cary F. Baynes (New York: Routledge, 2001), 112.

[2]Leo Tolstoy, *A Confession, The Gospel in Brief, and What I Believe*, trans. Aylmer Maude (New York: Oxford University Press, 1940), 17.

RICHARD

Drop the Mask; Get Real!

Scripture

By the grace of God I am what I am, and his grace toward me has not been in vain. On the contrary, I worked harder than any of them—though it was not I, but the grace of God that is with me (1 Cor. 15:10).

*A*s I consider my earlier life, I realize that satisfying my father's expectations and pleasing others robbed me of being myself. I wore a mask. Jung called this mask a *persona* and compared it to the role an actor must play when preparing for the stage. This "false" self implies that we learn our lines, follow the script, and play the role as we face the audience. When we play the role, we tend to forget who we really are, just as the mask becomes stuck to the actor's face, hiding the true face. I acted well many years, following the script written by my father—to continue the family tradition as a minister.

I spent many years building a "self" to satisfy others' desires for my life. Deep down I wondered if I was anything at all. As the years passed, I became stuck in my role and finally pursued a road less traveled and became a counselor/writer. It took hard work to walk away from the demands of my family of origin, but I knew I wasn't defrocked, only unsuited.

In my later years I came to embrace the exciting freedom of being who I really was. I could drop the mask I wore, dismantle old roles to find a deeper, more authentic self. I no longer had any need to stand out, achieve, or be better than anyone else. Yet even in the retirement community where I live, residents identified me in my role as pastor. Richard Rohr notes that some people call this "the crab bucket syndrome."[1] You want to get out of the bucket, but the other crabs keep pulling you in. In these later years I have moved beyond family and tradition to find my own soul and destiny apart from my Mom and Dad's desires for me.

I no longer concern myself with meeting others' expectations or desiring approval outside myself. I resonate with the words of poet May Sarton, who at age seventy wrote, "I am more myself than I have ever been."[2] I can identify with the apostle Paul whose earlier life as a Pharisee, a zealot for the law, made him intolerant of all others. Only when Christ met him on the road to Damascus did he drop the Pharisee role and become a "new creation." In writing to the church at Philippi, Paul recounted all his former achievements but then wrote, "Yet whatever gains I had, these I have come to regard as loss because of Christ" (Phil. 3:7). Now Paul could say, "By the grace of God I am what I am." He considered his past years of achievement under the law as loss for the "surpassing value of knowing Christ Jesus my Lord" (Phil. 3:8).

We might liken aging to attending a masquerade party. We have come wearing our masks to please others, paper people on parade. As we enter old age and face physical frailty, it is like midnight at the party. The lights dim; the audience dwindles; and we acknowledge the nearness of death. Now is the time to take off the masks, be vulnerable, and be who we are.

Reflection

- What roles have you played to please others and gain approval?
- How have you been able to move beyond your parents' desires for your life and find your "true" self? How does that make you feel now?

- How do you take advantage of the freedom to be who you are?
- How could you create a simpler lifestyle with time for prayer, meditation, and service?

[1]See Richard Rohr, *Falling Upward: A Spirituality for the Two Halves of Life* (San Francisco: Jossey-Bass, 2011), 83.

[2]May Sarton, *At Seventy: A Journal* (New York: W. W. Norton & Company, 1984), 10.

Richard

A Hard Thing to Be

Scripture

Then Jesus told his disciples, "If any want to become my followers, let them deny themselves and take up their cross and follow me. For those who want to save their life will lose it, and those who lose their life for my sake will find it" (Matt. 16:24-25).

SELF-CENTEREDNESS COMES with being human. Consider how many times we speak or act using the words *I, me, mine.* That number increases in old age when we no longer work and have more time on our hands.

Jesus said to the disciples, "If you want to be my follower, you must deny yourself" (AP). Jesus' request goes beyond denying material things to giving up the ego, the self that claims undue time and concern with *our* interests, desires, and needs.

Older people seem to have an inordinate need for attention. Preoccupation with our bodies heightens as health becomes a primary concern. Naturally we expect to be the center of attention. After serving others for years, we believe it is time to be served and have *our* needs met. In my retirement dining room some residents talk endlessly about themselves and their families.

I have to be careful about seeing this preoccupation with self in others, since the negative qualities we see in others are present within ourselves. I fear that in our later years we become more of what Carl Jung called "our shadow." Our shadow reflects what we refuse to see in ourselves and often project onto other people. The more we live out of our shadow self, the less capable we are of becoming our true self. The shadow self promotes a double blindness, keeping us from seeing our best self and that of others. As Jesus said, "If then the light in you is darkness, how great is the darkness! "(Matt. 6:23).

One way I have found to deny my ego is to be with people with Alzheimer's disease and other forms of dementia. They will never know my name and rarely offer affirmation. I simply am there for them, caring about them, as I try to engage them in conversation. In these moments I forget myself and think only of these souls.

The apostle Paul addressed the issue of selfless living in words to the church at Philippi, "Let the same mind be in you that was in Christ Jesus, who, though he was in the form of God, did not regard equality with God as something to be exploited, but emptied himself, taking the form of a slave" (Phil. 2:5-7). The lives of the great saints bear witness to this denial of ego. They show how God's love draws us from the egocentric self to a self in Christ. God calls us every day to selfless living in a needy world.

Reflection

- Take a few moments to bring to awareness needs other than your own. Make a list of these needs, and consider ways you might address them.
- The next time you sit at the table with family members or friends, practice restraining your speech and listen to what others are saying.
- How hard is it for you to keep your mind from formulating a response when a person is talking to you?
- How can you convince yourself that "just" listening is a gift to the other person?

GATEWAY 4
Living In and Out of Community

Now you are the body of Christ and individually members of it.

—1 CORINTHIANS 12:27

RICHARD

Created for Community

Scripture

How very good and pleasant it is
    when kindred live together in unity! (Ps. 133:1).

[All who believed] devoted themselves to the apostles' teaching
and fellowship, to the breaking of bread and the prayers
(Acts 2:42).

*T*HE FIRST TIME God said, "It is not good," came at the dawn
of Creation: "It is not good that the man should be alone" (Gen.
2:18). God created us for community. But we cannot live successfully in community until we learn to live with ourselves.

In my earlier years I put forward an extroverted facade driven
by my need for approval. I played the role of the good minister.
Now I find myself more of an introvert. I like to be with people in
limited doses and then retreat for solitude. I prefer a small number of close friends to social engagements with many people.

All my life I have sought a blessed community like the early
church in the book of Acts. The early church had no buildings or
organizational structure. It was a dynamic fellowship of kindred
souls who shared a common life. Luke, the early-church histo-
rian used the word *together* several times in describing the early
church. "All who believed were together" (Acts 2:44). "Day by
day, as they spent much time together" (Acts 2:46). When Paul
wrote letters to young churches, he addressed disciples who met
in homes scattered across a city. The letters were first read to one
house church and then passed on to others.

I have experienced difficulty in finding community in traditional structures. Sixty years ago when I began my ministry, I had a lovers' quarrel with the institutional church. I urged that what we needed was not a conversion *to* the church but a conversion *in* the church. Through many years I have noted an institutional church decline. I appreciate the story of the medieval artist who painted the face of Jesus rather red. When asked why he did that, he replied, "Because Jesus must blush to see what we have done to the church!"

At times I want to stand up in the church I attend and shout, "No one died who didn't rise again!" I wonder if the best community might entail a small group of committed disciples who practice the presence of Christ.

I have found a touch of called-togetherness in this retirement community. The residents come from different cultures and faiths, but what binds us is our common vulnerability and common faith in God. We guard one another's privacy, yet share a common life. We eat together, worship together, play together, mourn together, and reach out to each other when we hurt.

In some ways the residents in this retirement facility form a "natural monastery." All of us have relinquished ownership of private property, scaled down our possessions to a minimum, and practiced self-denial in order to grow in our relationship to one another and to God. We have abandoned former roles and attachments while gaining a community of acceptance and love. As we share our mutual woes, we experience a community where "if one member suffers, all suffer together with it" (1 Cor. 12:26).

Reflection

- Make a list of some of the religious communities in your life. How did they help you come closer to God and other members of the community? How did they hinder you?

- When you have experienced crises in your life, to whom did you turn for support?
- How might living in a retirement facility foster true community? Where else do you find that kind of community?

Richard

The Inner Circle

Scripture

"I do not call you servants any longer, because the servant does not know what the master is doing, but I have called you friends" (John 15:15).

Jesus showed love and compassion to all, but he had an inner circle of friends. Jesus called twelve men to be his disciples. He traveled with them, lived with them, and depended on them to carry on the ministry. Three of those disciples—Peter, James, and John—were with him in crucial moments of his ministry (Transfiguration, Gethsemane). Luke tells us that women like Mary Magdalene, Joanna, Susanna, and others financed Jesus' ministry (Luke 8:2-3). Jesus often stayed at the home of friends like Mary, Martha, and Lazarus of Bethany. During the tumultuous events of Holy Week, spending time with this family strengthened Jesus to face the ordeal in Jerusalem.

As I entered my later years, I discovered that I had fewer acquaintances but an inner circle of friends. I am available to members of this community retirement when they seek my help; I listen to their concerns. Yet, I spend most of my time with a small circle of friends: my wife, my daughter and her family, and several residents. This circle includes Bill, a rather eccentric man, whom some ignore because of his strange ways. It includes Ed and Louise, a devoted couple, whose only son died. It includes Gertrude, whose saintly life sheds a light that comes from the soul.

The Celtic tradition offers a beautiful understanding of friendship. The Celts called it *anam cara*, a Gaelic word for "soul friend." With soul friends you share your innermost self. On the night before his death, Jesus called his disciples "friends." They were no longer servants, bound to take orders as slaves obey the master's will. They became his soul friends who did his will out of love. I have experienced that close communion with residents here—particularly with the special few.

This inner circle reminds me of the words of the Quaker Thomas R. Kelly:

> Within the wider Fellowship emerges the special circle of a few on whom, for each of us, a particular emphasis of nearness has fallen. These are our special gift and task. These we "carry" by inward, wordless prayer. . . . It is as if the boundaries of our self were enlarged, as if we were within them and as if they were within us.[1]

The participants had just sung "What a Friend We Have in Jesus" in a worship service for people with dementia. I stopped the service and asked those gathered (most of whom never spoke), "What is a friend?" Maggie looked at me, and replied, "I am your friend." In that grace moment Maggie became part of my special circle.

Reflection

- Draw a circle on a piece of paper; write your name in the center of a circle.
- Think of an inner circle of friends who have touched your life. Write their names around the outer edge of the circle.
- Now imagine those people standing at different points on the circumference of the circle.
- Look at them and say a prayer of gratitude for the way they have touched your life.

[1] Thomas R. Kelly, *A Testament of Devotion* (New York: Harper & Row, 1941), 85–86.

RICHARD

Stability at Last

Scripture

Therefore put on the full armor of God, so that when the day of evil comes, you may be able to stand your ground, and after you have done everything, to stand (<u>Eph. 6:13</u>, NIV).

*W*HEN MY WIFE AND I ENTERED this retirement community we voluntarily committed to live here "till death do us part." That was a real switch for me. I had spent my earlier years always on the move, thinking the "next" place would bring me happiness. In my mind I was always elsewhere—seldom in the place where I stood. My daydreams usually began with those insidious words "if only. . . ." I went through fifteen changes of residence before moving to this community.

I had an opportunity to teach Bible at Davidson College but suffered from a Jonah Complex, running away from possible greatness out of fear of failure. Like the prophet Jonah who fled to Tarshish rather than answer God's call, I chose smaller, safer situations rather than venturing out into deeper waters. Yet, I did not find peace either in constant moving or in places of refuge.

I have discovered that a meaningful life comes not in rushing from one place to another but in <u>committing to life where we find ourselves.</u> Stability denotes <u>perseverance with patience.</u> "Somebody asked Antony [the noted desert monk], 'What shall I do in order to please God?' He replied, 'Do what I tell you, which is this: wherever you go, keep God in mind; whatever you do, follow the example of holy Scripture; wherever you are, stay there and do not move away in a hurry.'"[1] So I have accepted this particular community, this place, and the people in this place as a way to God.

The apostle Paul learned stability in his later years. Imprisoned in a Roman jail, he wrote, "I have learned to be content with whatever I have" (Phil. 4:11). Earlier he had dreamed of taking the gospel to Spain, but now he has learned to be content with existing in a cold, Roman jail. Paul, at peace within himself, could affirm, "I can do all things through him who strengthens me" (Phil. 4:13).

Stability comes from a Latin word that means "firmness of resolve," "steadfastness." We refuse to run away, acknowledging that we will remain for the long haul. For older people in this drip-dry, disposable society, stability becomes a priority—a belief that we belong and have roots.

I keep the words of the Chinese philosopher Lao Tzu on a card by my computer: "Without going out of my door I can know all things on earth. Without looking out of my window, I can know the ways of heaven. For the further one travels the less one knows. The sage therefore arrives without traveling, sees all without looking" (*Tao Te Ching*, chapter 47). I am living out those words, settled in this community.

Reflection

- How many times have you moved in your life? Did those moves bring happiness?
- In what community did you find the greatest joy?
- What kind of a community would you choose to live out your final years? Retirement community? Staying at home and maintaining ties to your church family ? Or what?

¹Benedicta Ward, trans., *The Desert Fathers: Sayings of the Early Christian Monks* (New York: Penguin Books, 2003), 3.

RICHARD

Welcoming Neighbors and Strangers

Scripture

"Then the righteous will answer him, 'Lord, . . . when was it that we saw you a stranger and welcomed you . . . ?' . . . 'Truly I tell you, just as you did it to one of the least of these who are members of my family, you did it to me'" (Matt. 25:37-38, 40).

𝓛IVING IN A RETIREMENT COMMUNITY means that every day brings opportunities to welcome strangers and help neighbors. We might write the words of Saint Benedict on our hearts: "All guests who present themselves are to be welcomed as Christ, for he himself will say: *I was a stranger and you welcomed me*."[1] Residents are called to awareness of new people who need our welcome, as well as those who walk our halls and live here. "When did we see you, Christ?" Every day in the life of this community.

Welcome strangers. I know what it feels like to be a stranger. As a child I was bullied by neighborhood gangs, always the one outside the circle. As an adult I became an outsider when I sided with African American people in a racist Southern town—which cost me my job. The only person who bid me good-bye was an African American janitor whom I had befriended.

I came to this retirement community as a stranger. We moved here to be near our daughter. Unlike other residents who came from nearby communities and maintained friendships, we knew no one except our daughter and her family. I believe that every time a new person enters this community, it is Christ who comes.

Christ comes in a new resident whose children have left her here, and she feels lost and alienated. Christ is the person who fell in the parking lot and broke her hip but has no family to call on for help. I find Christ in the faces of people I meet every day. I see Christ in the struggles of staff members, whose lives can be burdened with trying to please so many "old people." Christ is especially present in the lives of people with dementia who sit in silence, hoping someone will stop and speak to them. Christ comes in the widow, still overcome with grief, who lives alone, never making friends and who sits at your table in the dining room. The distinguishing mark of a spiritual person is turning strangers into friends.

Making friends in this community has its heartaches, for many die and leave us. In our later years we relinquish many losses, yet we never relinquish the sense of being called by God to love God by loving neighbor. Growing old brings illness, diminished capacities, and increasing frailty. Some elders retreat into self-absorption. As Christians, we never outgrow our vocation to bring Christ to others. At the last day our judgment will hinge on whether we welcomed the stranger as if that person were Christ himself. This community provides an opportunity to mirror the words of John Fawcett's hymn, "We share each other's woes, our mutual burdens bear; and often for each other flows the sympathizing tear."

Reflection

- Can you remember a time when you were a stranger? Did someone welcome you? If not, how did you feel?
- How can you practice daily the words of Mother Teresa, "We do not need to carry out grand things in order to show a great love for God and for our neighbor"?[2]

[1]Fry, *Rule of St. Benedict*, 51.

[2]Mother Teresa, *No Greater Love*, ed. Becky Benenate and Joseph Durepos (Novato, CA: New World Library, 2002), 26.

Jane

Learning Interdependence: To Receive Is to Give

Scripture

Then [Jesus] poured water into a basin and began to wash the disciples' feet. . . . He came to Simon Peter, who said to him, "Lord, are you going to wash my feet?" Jesus answered, "You do not know now what I am doing, but later you will understand." Peter said to him, "You will never wash my feet." Jesus answered, "Unless I wash you, you have no share with me" (John 13:5-8).

ONE SERIOUS DIMINISHMENT of aging comes when we reach the point of needing personal care provided by complete strangers—or even our child. Most people dread the day when they will require help with such personal tasks as toileting, bathing, and dressing. Some of the people who feel that to live to be 120 would be a curse say they would rather die than "endure that indignity." But is it really an indignity? Did we consider it an indignity when we were cared for in the same way during our infancy and early childhood? Was it an indignity for Jesus to wash Peter's feet? Was it an indignity for Peter to allow his feet to be washed?

We often interpret the account of Jesus' washing his disciples' feet as Jesus' desire that we strip ourselves of condescending pretensions and humble ourselves to help those in need. (An example of the maxim *to give is better than to receive.*) That's only half of the story. It *is* good to give, but sometimes the act of receiving is a greater gift. It takes even more humility to put ourselves in the lower place, allowing ourselves to be cared for without complaint. Jesus refused to allow Peter to work with him any longer if he chose not to allow his feet to be washed. The issue is one of power and powerlessness; who is one-up and who is one-down. Unless we are willing to be one-down—to be the recipient of care—at least once in a while, we have no business demanding to be the person in power, always doing the caregiving. This mutuality is what interdependence entails.

How can a person who is ill, who is entirely dependent on others for such intimate care, be the giver? First of all, an attitude of gratitude rather than of anger, resentment, or even embarrassment toward the caregiver is an enormous gift. I have friends who provide home care, giving frail people baths in their own home. Often they report the meanness of some of their clients toward them. My friends realize that the meanness denotes an attempt to control the situation, to let the caregiver know that the care receiver is simply enduring an undignified process and would much rather be doing it himself or herself. But understanding nasty behavior doesn't make it easier for the caregiver to endure it. Understood or not, such behavior wears down patience! Going a step further, an attitude of interested kindness toward service providers is also a gift. Asking about their lives rather than focusing on self is a way to serve them.

In essence, care receivers can give significant gifts of encouraging words, a genuine smile, a heartfelt thank-you, and a listening ear—and make a huge difference in the quality of their caregivers' lives. A friend suffering from Parkinson's disease was placed, much against his will, into a nursing home. He asked God how he could best serve God in this situation. The response he sensed was this: "love them with my love." So he decided to act on God's answer by expressing gratitude for things he had formerly complained about; the results went far beyond his hopes. The caregivers expressed amazement at his thanking them for services like giving him a bath; one commented that his gratitude enabled her to endure with grace the negativity of the patient in the next room.

Reflection

- As Christians we are called to be God's presence in the world, no matter where in the world or in what condition we find ourselves. God's love, given to the world by those who love God, can transform a hell into a heaven. Could you think of your time in rehab or the nursing home or even receiving care from strangers in your own home as a mission field?
- You will encounter people who greatly need God's love. Into what negative situation can you pour God's love? How can you do it?

JANE

Possessed by Possessions: Owned by Stuff

Scripture

Jesus said [to the rich young man], "If you wish to be perfect, go, sell your possessions, and give the money to the poor, and you will have treasure in heaven; then come, follow me." When the young man heard this word, he went away grieving, for he had many possessions (Matt. 19:21-22).

𝒀EARS AGO A FRIEND said to me (as I was trying to convince him to buy a small, inexpensive boat so he could canoe with us), "No thanks, I'll rent. The more I possess, the more my possessions possess me. I want freedom from 'stuff'!" His words stunned me. I'd never thought about being possessed by my possessions. I lean toward collecting. Before retiring, I liked the sight of an overstuffed clothes closet—even when I could no longer fit into the clothes! I enjoyed what I called "shopping in my own closet!" Now that I no longer have to dress for work each day, I'm having an opposite experience. Rather than giving me pleasure, the sight of the overfilled walk-in closet seems to suffocate me. I want to get rid of three-fourths of the stuff; but aside from a desultory donation to Goodwill every few months, I can't seem to let go. I have finally realized that I do not possess the clothes. I have allowed them to possess me, and I am holding myself in a kind of bondage.

I sense a connection with the young man in Matthew 19 who had so much stuff that possessed him that he couldn't move on in his life with Jesus. And I am just starting to realize what Jesus is getting at here. In my earlier years I used to believe this passage was about an elite vocation for a few special people—Jesus' invitation to someone he found worthy enough to become a missionary, minister, priest, religious. Jesus was calling this person to follow him in a very special way in the institutional church, and the invitee needed to leave his/her material belongings behind in order to follow freely. And that may be a valid interpretation. Now that I am older, however, I am beginning to understand this passage in a more universal way, a way pertinent to those of us in later life as well as those beginning their generative lives.

My first new insight into this passage came when I tried to help an older woman in my congregation decide to move to an assisted living home. She knew she needed assistance, and she really wanted to go! She was bored, lonely, and overwhelmed by the ongoing needs of the two-story, four-bedroom home in which she'd lived for the past fifty years and had raised her children. She had chosen a new first-rate facility where a number of her friends already lived—two-thirds of her Sunday school class and her best bridge partners. She couldn't wait to go, but she couldn't make the move. She was paralyzed. Why? She couldn't part with the treasures she had collected over the years, many of which she had inherited from grandparents and parents. She was possessed by the multitude of gifts she had been given by her husband, children and grandchildren, let alone the things she had bought herself!

One gerontologist has suggested that as we age we externalize our identity into things. For example, we buy an inexpensive mug to remind us of a vacation we have enjoyed. Every time we use it, we remember fondly the vacation and the people we were with. Over time, with the fading of our brain power, the object becomes an external memory, like an external hard drive now available to increase the storage capacity of our computers. Over time we begin to fear that in letting go of the object we will lose the memory and thus a part of our very selves.

I am beginning to think that what Jesus was telling the young man and all of us who want to follow him is this: "Get rid of the stuff that has created a false identity for you. It's OK to forget the memories those items represented. Find your identity, your true self, in me rather than in a teacup, a fishing rod, or even a house. In doing this you will find a better treasure, heaven, now."

Reflection

- What possessions keep you from living a lifestyle that is more appropriate to your needs at this time?
- What stuff is defining who you are?
- How does attachment to your "things" keep you from living in community with people?
- Do you invest more of your energy in caring for your possessions than in your relationships?

JANE

Becoming a Christ-gift

Scripture

It is no longer I who live, but it is Christ who lives in me (Gal. 2:20).

Jesus answered [Judas], "Those who love me will keep my word, and my Father will love them, and we will come to them and make our home with them" (John 14:23).

"Remember, I am with you always, to the end of the age." (Matt. 28:20).

"If you love me, you will keep my commandments. And I will ask the Father, and he will give you another Advocate, to be with you forever" (John 14:15-16).

How odd it is that we so often think of the Father, Jesus, and the Spirit as being "out there" somewhere, distant or at least external to ourselves. We pray to God "in heaven" as though heaven were some far-distant place. We pray and ask God to be with us, yet God *is* with us, within us, throughout us! We try to imitate Jesus by asking, "What would Jesus do?" Jesus tells his friends that if they love him, they will do what he desires, which is to love one another. And when they love one another, the Trinity—Father, Jesus, and Spirit—will make a home within them. That will transform them into Christ-gifts for one another.

What a mind-boggling realization! With God residing within me, my vocation, my calling, my responsibility, task—whatever you call it—is to allow myself to be a Christ-gift to everybody!

Think about the significance of this reality. Can we even imagine what would happen in and to the world (let alone our families) if every Christian fully realized that we are enabled at *all* times and in *all* circumstances to let Christ love others through us? When we pray for someone, we often ask God to help that person. But if God lives within us, then the task involves our being the visible presence of the God within. We allow God to love and help and do whatever needs to be done through us!

What does being a Christ-gift mean for our lives in the Last Third? It means that in *all circumstances* our lives will remain meaningful to us and be of use to others. We might consider the act of being a Christ-gift to the world as our work, our calling, our vocation for this time of life in whatever condition we find ourselves. Know that this work is God's—the work of bringing God's realm to fruition. When we pray, "Thy kingdom come, thy will be done," we choose to participate in the world's transformation.

Anna, a woman in her late nineties, lives alone and depends on weekly visits from home-care nurses to change the dressings on a leg wound that will not heal. She is sight-impaired *and* hearing-impaired, as well as diabetic. She is the last living member of her family. Yet she is neither lonely nor alone. At least one person visits each day, sometimes two or more. They flock to her because she allows Christ to listen lovingly to them through her. Her many friends of all ages know that Anna always has time and a nonjudgmental listening ear for them. They leave feeling better than when they arrived.

Anna does nothing herself. She brings her awareness of God within to the fore and allows God's presence to love her visitor through her, frail as she is. Despite her physical losses, frailty, and even pain, she remains one of the happiest people I have ever encountered. We all have this option if we choose to be Christ-gifts to the world!

One simple way to begin the practice of being a Christ-gift is to smile more often. A smile can demonstrate kindness, encouragement, friendliness, love. It can break through resistances, sadness, even anger. It makes the recipient feel better, and we feel better when we smile. A friend tells me that she always answers her business (and home) telephone with a smile, even before she knows who it is. She says that her smile is her face-lift, and it lifts up others as well. And it doesn't cost a penny!

Reflection

- In your current experience, where is God?
- Do you ever realize that the Trinity lives within you? If you could grasp this reality, really believe this, how would your life change?
- How might the world change if we enabled Christ to live through us?
- Have you ever thought of smiling more often? Try it, and see what happens.

GATEWAY 5
Prayer and Contemplation

—◈—

Pray without ceasing.

1 Thessalonians 5:17

RICHARD

Meditate Not Vegetate

Scripture

"Whenever you pray, go into your room and shut the door and pray to your Father who is in secret; and your Father who sees in secret will reward you" (Matt. 6:6).

*T*HESE EXTENDED YEARS of life God has given me are a rich gift. I don't have to worry about job performance or meeting deadlines (except for writing assignments). No one expects me to run a marathon or start a new career. My mantra now is, "Stop doing and focus on being." How shall I spend these bonus years? I refuse to buy into the culture that equates busyness with importance. Many retirees when asked, "What are you doing now?" reply, "I'm staying busy." I avoid that frenetic lifestyle. If people love me, they will love me for who I am, not what I do.

However, this free time brings the temptation to while away the days playing games and simply vegetating. The great temptations of old age are to whine, to decline, and to recline. I have chosen not to spend the gift of these years in busyness or meaningless activity. Like Mary of Bethany, I prefer "the better part," the contemplative life, experiencing the inner sanctuary of the soul.

The contemplative life implies a stillness and quietness of our souls, which are liberated from the need to achieve or be more than we are. As the psalmist expressed it, "I have calmed and quieted my soul, like a weaned child with its mother" (Ps. 131:2). I rest in the embrace of my Parent.

Even this delightful freedom of my later years demands discipline. The temptation lurks in the shadow to fritter away this precious gift of time doing that which cannot satisfy the deep longings of my heart. I need a place and a time for prayer and meditation if I am to pray constantly and keep God alive in my heart. Jesus cautioned us, "The gate is narrow and the road is hard that leads to life" (Matt. 7:14). I have the role models in women and men who have walked through this narrow gate and found life. But the path is not mine until I embrace it for myself.

In the Sermon on the Mount Jesus taught his disciples to "go into your room and shut the door and pray to your Father who is in secret." Fortunately, I live in a community where I am only a few steps from our chapel; I can go there and pray. In my small apartment, I have created a "cell" marked by mementos of pilgrimages to Tintern Abbey in Wales and the island of Iona. Prayer and spiritual books put me in touch with monks and mystics who show the way, who have walked the hard road that leads to life.

I also know that I can "pray without ceasing" and realize God's presence wherever I am without being lost in my illusions. By entering the narrow gate of a disciplined life of prayer, I discover the true meaning of life in the later years.

Reflection

- Go to a quiet place and spend fifteen minutes in prayer, as you meditate on these words:

  Be still and know that I am God
  Be still and know
  Be still
  Be

RICHARD

Silence, Please!

Scripture

For God alone my soul waits in silence,
    from him comes my salvation (Ps. 62:1).

The LORD was not in the earthquake; and after the earthquake
a fire, but the LORD was not in the fire; and after the fire a
sound of sheer silence (1 Kings 19:11-12).

*I*N OUR BUSY AND RUSHED culture, silence is rare and seldom
a priority. Many people perceive silence as aberrant behavior. Sitting in silence makes many people anxious. However, living in a
retirement community with no responsibility for maintaining a
home or managing a career frees up time to be still.

When I was a child, my parents sent me to a Quaker school
in Philadelphia. Seventy-five years later, I still relive those long
morning assemblies where we sat in silence until the Spirit moved
someone to speak. Even now I can feel the narrow, hard benches
and see everyone sitting together, symbolizing our unity in God.
As I gazed up at the sunlight streaming through the windows during those long stretches of silence, I began to know God's presence,
which has stayed with me throughout life. I learned to appreciate
Paul's words in Romans, "The Spirit helps us in our weakness; for
we do not know how to pray as we ought, but that very Spirit intercedes with sighs too deep for words" (Rom. 8:26).

The prophet Elijah, fleeing for his life, comes to Mount Horeb
and takes up residence in a cave. A wind of terrifying force, an
earthquake, and fire assaulted his senses. Elijah did not hear God
speak through these forces but in the "sound of sheer silence."

The psalmist knew where to find God, "For God alone my soul waits in silence" (Psalm 62:1). I now have the time to cultivate silence. Sometimes I sit in the chapel and simulate those Friends meetings of so long ago. I have also found that early morning and the last thing at night are optimum times to practice silence.

As the day ends, the darkness can seem overwhelming. One of my night rituals involves emptying everything out of my pockets and putting the contents on the dresser. This action helps me realize that I need to empty my mind of all distractions and embrace the silence of darkness. God can break through to me in the inner light as I remain quiet and still. I have also learned in the Last Third of life to avoid loud music, large crowds, and needless diversions. I find that silence and poetry have become a more natural voice. I have learned the truth of Thomas Keating's words, "Silence is God's first language."[1]

One lesson that people with dementia have taught me is the value of silence. Some of these souls never speak; but sitting with them, I become aware of God's presence; I restrain my speech and am still. A story from the desert fathers relates that a brother came to Abbot Moses, seeking a word from him. The abbot replied, "Go, and sit in your cell, and your cell will teach you everything."[2] I am learning now what that means.

Reflection
- Find a quiet spot somewhere. If you live in a retirement community, go to the chapel. Or, find a church in your neighborhood and spend some time in silence. Or, find a quiet place beside a lake or in a wooded area, and be silent.
- Record what you experience.

[1] Thomas Keating, *Intimacy with God* (New York: Crossroad, 1994), 55.
[2] Ward, *The Desert Fathers*, 10.

RICHARD

Solitary Refinement

Scripture

In the morning, while it was still very dark, [Jesus] got up and went out to a deserted place, and there he prayed (Mark 1:35).

ON MANY OCCASIONS, Jesus withdrew from the crowds or his own disciples to be alone with God. Mark tells us that at sundown one day, people brought their sick to Jesus to be healed. The next morning Jesus withdrew to a deserted place to be alone with God. Despite his busy life, Jesus took time for solitude. Luke tells us that after Jesus healed a man with leprosy, crowds gathered to hear him and be cured of their diseases. Jesus then withdrew to a deserted place to pray (Luke 5:16). In the Gospel of Matthew we read that Jesus, grieved by the death of his cousin John the Baptist, "withdrew from there in a boat to a desert place by himself" (14:13). Jesus understood the power of solitary refinement.

After I retired from the work world and then from too much volunteering, a quietness settled on my life. Now I realize that in our incessant need to talk, we miss out on the gifts of silence. Blaise Pascal noted that many of our problems derive from our inability to sit still in a room.[1] We feel pressured to fill our minds with endless thoughts. Eastern traditions have called the restlessness of our minds, the "monkey mind." Just as monkeys swing from tree to tree, our minds swing from one thought to the next.

Theologian Paul Tillich wrote, "Our language has widely sensed these two sides of [our] being alone. It has created the word 'loneliness' to express the pain of being alone. And it has created the word 'solitude' to express the glory of being alone."[2]

Even as our bodies become frail, moments spent with God in solitude nourish our souls and keep us young. Meister Eckhart, the German mystic, wrote (as translated and freely adapted by Matthew Fox),

> My soul is as young as the day it was created.
> Yes, and much younger!
> In fact, I am younger today than I was yesterday,
> and if I am not younger tomorrow than I am today,
> I would be ashamed of myself.
> People who dwell in God dwell in the eternal now.
> There, people can never grow old . . . . [3]

Instead of spending millions on potions and lotions to make us look younger, we can discover that devotion to the contemplative life brings a youth of soul that makes us vibrant and alive, despite what age may do to our bodies. Take time to be alone with God, for what else matters in these years and in the years to come?

Reflection

- Go outdoors alone, and find a flower of your liking.
- Concentrate on the flower, looking, smelling, touching it, realizing the flower is part of you and you are part of the flower.
- What comes to your mind when you do this? What feelings do you experience?

[1]Blaise Pascal, *Pensées and Other Writings*, trans. Honor Levi (New York: Oxford University Press, 1995), 44.

[2]Paul Tillich, *The Eternal Now* (New York: Charles Scribner's Sons, 1963), 17–18.

[3]Matthew Fox, trans., *Meditations with Meister Eckhart* (Santa Fe, NM: Bear & Company, 2005), 32.

Richard

Divine Reading

Scripture

She had a sister named Mary, who sat at the Lord's feet and listened to what he was saying. . . . "Mary has chosen the better part, which will not be taken away from her" (Luke 10:39, 42).

Lectio Divina ("divine reading") consists of reading words of scripture prayerfully. There are four movements in this "divine reading," and the image of eating helps us understand these different stages of "digesting" a text. *Reading* puts the food in our mouth; in *meditating* we chew the food, as we repeat the text again and again. We swallow the text by *praying* the words, which extracts its flavor, and through *contemplating* we enjoy God's presence which refreshes our soul, as food nourishes our bodies. This kind of divine reading helps us hear what God is saying to us now.

Mary of Bethany offers a classic example of "divine reading" as she sits quietly at Jesus' feet and digests his words. Her holy listening leads to a deep level of contemplation and prayer. Jesus rebukes Martha not so much for her hostess activity but for her frenetic busyness that has made her tense and anxious. Both sisters reflect a way of prayer. Martha, busy and bustling, prays through her activity. Mary chooses the quieter, more reflective life, devoted to listening to Jesus.

I have never thought that Jesus' words to Martha were a criticism of kitchen duty or getting things done. Brother Lawrence practiced the presence of God scrubbing pots and pans in the monastery kitchen. I interpret Jesus' words to Martha as a warning not to be so distracted with household chores that she forgets God.

I can relate to Martha, especially in my years of work, when I was pushed and prodded by clock and calendar to get things done. I still get distracted and at times anxious. Even as I "pray through" this Bible story, the phone rings. I heard the voice of a distraught woman whose husband has Alzheimer's disease. She is at her wits' end and asks about the Alzheimer's support group. For me, prayer includes not only alone time with God but being present with persons in need. I prayed as I listened to that woman and offered support and help. Martha lost sight of the joy of delighting in Jesus. Her preoccupation with being the perfect hostess overshadowed the joy of being with the perfect guest.

So, like Mary, I withdraw from the cell phone, computer, and other electronic marvels and spend time in "divine reading" of the story. I identify with both sisters. I am Martha in my need to stay active as an older person; I am Mary in seeking to be single-minded in my devotion to God. Divine reading means I need to find that vital balance between activity and contemplation.

Reflection

- Set aside some time to practice *lectio divina*.
1. Read Luke 10:38-41, then reread it.
2. Imagine that you are an unseen guest in the house at Bethany and overhear the conversations among Jesus, Martha, and Mary.
3. Pray the story, asking God to show you its meaning for you now. Then sit, quietly nourished by God's presence in your life.

- You might want to record your experience in your journal.

JANE

Accepting Uncertainty

Scripture

Come now, you who say, "Today or tomorrow we will go to such and such a town and spend a year there, doing business and making money." Yet you do not even know what tomorrow will bring. What is your life? For you are a mist that appears for a little while and then vanishes. Instead you ought to say," If the Lord wishes, we will live and do this or that" (James 4:13-15).

B y the time we reach the Last Third of our lives, most of us know that life holds no certainties for us as individuals, for our families, for society, or even for the planet. We turn on the TV and see individual lives snuffed out and families all over the world destroyed by the destructive forces of earthquakes and tsunamis, by war, by disease, by such chance events as a collision with a sleepy driver. Yet we live as though we ourselves will escape death. And we continue to act as if we control our lives. When we face failure to "do our business"—whatever that is at the moment—we feel let down by the unfairness of life and sometimes even resort to adult tantrums.

Living with the illusion that we have control over our lives helps us fend off the anxiety of knowing that someday we will die. We create little worlds around ourselves and put all our efforts into decorating them with things that make us secure—like annuities, long-term care insurance, reverse mortgages, regular colonoscopies and mammograms, diets high in fiber and antioxidants, and at least thirty minutes of exercise five times per week. And if we're not succeeding in following these regimens, we succumb to guilt!

(I am not saying we shouldn't do these things, but we shouldn't rely on them to keep us safe from eventual death.)

After eight rounds of chemotherapy to treat non-Hodgkin's lymphoma, I was diagnosed with congestive heart failure—the result of damage done by the chemo not the lymphoma. I was not too perturbed by that second dire diagnosis and the two medications it required to maintain cardiac stability, dismissing it with, "Well, I am just grateful that I am alive!" However, when my insurance company informed me that they wanted to install a computerized device connected to my physician's office that would monitor my blood pressure and weight every morning at the same time, I descended into my version of an adult tantrum. It went like this: "I don't want to be told what to do! This will interfere with my daily schedule. What if I don't want to get up at the same time every day? The monitoring device is going to disturb my computer connection, and I can't afford to mess it up because I'm writing a book for The Upper Room that has to be finished in eight weeks!" And the final denial, "I don't have the real version of congestive heart failure. My weight is stable; I don't get edematous; and my blood pressure is low, not high. I don't need the daily monitoring. I'm not as bad off as some other people I know who have this diagnosis!" Translation: "I don't want to give up control of my life to anyone—even if it is for my own good!"

How can we respond to this incessant desire to be in charge of our lives? How can we "let go and let God?" Adopting the contemplative attitude of surrender is key. We are taught from an early age that we need to take control of our lives, so it is not easy to see the value in changing that mind-set. But willingness to give up the illusion of control, willingness to relinquish the need to control—our own lives and the lives of others—is the first step toward being able to say, "If the Lord wishes, we will live and do this or that." We can begin this process by repeating as prayer throughout the day Jesus' words from the cross, "Into your hands I commend my spirit." Sooner or later our behavior will follow our prayer.

Reflection

- How do you create the illusion that you are in control of your life?
- How does your illusion interfere with your physical, mental, social, or spiritual well-being?
- How can you let go of the illusion and face your reality?

JANE

Savoring Your Life

Scripture

In the last days it will be, God declares,
that I will pour out my Spirit upon all flesh,
    and your sons and your daughters shall prophesy,
and your young men shall see visions,
    and your old men shall dream dreams (Acts 2:17).

SOME PEOPLE COULD rightfully call me a drudge, always thinking about my next chore or obligation. But I have definitely improved since marrying my husband, Ron. He is full of joy and fun with a deep appreciation of each day he is alive! I have recognized the need to "lighten up" since March 28, 1973. That's the date of one of my most significant, life-changing dreams.

I was living in the Mojave Desert at the time and hating every moment of it. In the early morning of 3/28/73 I dreamed that I had died and was about to face my life judgment to determine my worthiness for heaven. I walked into a modern high-rise building and was escorted to the top floor. The top floor housed an elegant, spacious penthouse with an outer foyer where a secretary sat at her desk. She rose, took my arm, and guided me through a heavy walnut door into the main room. She left me, saying, "He'll be with you shortly, just wait here." I stood and looked around. I was on the top floor of the building; the room was surrounded by floor-to-ceiling windows that looked out on a city in all directions and flooded the room with light. Along the walls television screens displayed different scenes. A tall man who seemed unaware of my presence went from screen to screen, avidly watching what was happening on each. I couldn't see them all, but on one a woman was delivering a baby; on another a ball game was taking place; on another a surgeon was in the operating room. At each screen the man acted like a cheerleader, saying to the woman, "You can do it, keep going!" and to the ball players, "Fantastic playing, all of you!" and to the surgeon, "Good job, I'm with you!" What struck me was the total attention he gave each and the enthusiasm with which he encouraged everyone he watched. Suddenly he realized I was in the room, so he turned his attention to me, smiling widely.

"Sit down," the man said in a welcoming voice, pointing to a chair across from his desk. As I sat gingerly on the chair, he plopped down on his own desk chair and put his feet up on the desk, crossing them at the ankles and leaning back. He was wearing well-worn tennis shoes with a small hole in both soles, and I couldn't take my eyes off them. When I did I realized that he was smiling at me as if amused. I noticed that he was thin, with dark hair cut short and a closely trimmed beard. He was wearing a white turtleneck shirt with khaki slacks—and white socks! I was shocked to realize that this was Jesus—unlike any Jesus I had ever seen in a painting or imagined in my meditation.

After a moment of watching me, the man leaned forward and said enthusiastically, "So, tell me, how did you like it?" "What do you mean, 'how did I like it?'" I asked nervously—and a tiny bit crossly. "How did you like your life?" he responded kindly, but with genuine curiosity. He really wanted to know if I liked my life. I wasn't expecting this question. I was expecting to see some kind of life review and be judged on my behavior, and I remained speechless for a few seconds. When I came to myself I responded in a way I can't quite believe I had the audacity to do. "Not all that much," I said. I complained to him that I was angry that my parents had died when I was a teenager and that I had spent my life trying to be good enough to get into heaven. I then listed all the joys I had given up, all the duties I had performed, all the work I had done to make myself "worthy." I initially married the denominationally acceptable man (not Ron), took a job as a social worker instead of being the biology teacher I wanted to be. I went on and on listing all the earthly joys I had forgone in order to earn the promise of a much better life in heaven. I had thought this would please him, but as I listed one thing after another, I saw his joy wane. His smile left, replaced by an expression of deep sadness. "I am so sorry, Janie," he said, "but you can't come here yet. You're not ready. Heaven is very much like your life on earth, but much more so! Because you haven't learned to savor, to deeply appreciate the life you have lived, just doing your 'duty' to get to a better place, you wouldn't even be able to experience heaven as heaven. You don't have the ability yet. You must go back and learn to savor your life before you can come back and enjoy heaven."

At that point I woke up. The dream disturbed me intensely. How could Jesus not be interested in my "service record" and in the sacrifices I had made to be with him later in heaven? Certainly the *real* Jesus would not be concerned about whether or not I had enjoyed my life, would he? After hours of trying to discern the meaning of the dream, I finally decided it represented a temptation to stray from my duty. I recorded the dream on paper, slipped it into an envelope, sealed it, put it away, and refused to consider the truth of the dream for the next twenty years—until I almost died in a collision with a tractor-trailer truck on October 2, 1993.

The accident forced me to reevaluate my life. The reality, the truth, of the dream emerged. I decided to explore its truth for me. I am still exploring.

Reflection

- What about you? Do you really appreciate the gift of your life and the gifts of your life?

JANE

Corresponding with God

Scripture

"Whenever you pray, go into your room and shut the door and pray to your Father who is in secret; and your Father who sees in secret will reward you" (Matt. 6:6).

"Ask, and it will be given you; search, and you will find; knock, and the door will be opened for you. For everyone who asks receives, and everyone who searches finds" (Matt. 7:7-10).

I SEEM TO EXPERIENCE what I call "seasons" of prayer, different ways of praying for the spiritual season I happen to be in. In my winter spiritual season I don't want to pray at all. God seems to be an artifact of my imagination, and speaking to God and trying to listen feels like a futile exercise. Formal prayer, reading the Psalms, participating in the rituals of the church community, worship and liturgy, attending Sunday school carry me along during this trying time. In my prayer springtime I look forward to praying, eagerly anticipating the times alone with God or delving into scripture or reading a new spiritual book. In the summer season of prayer I rest in God in a more contemplative, wordless way. And in the fall I write in my journal. But in times of crisis or confusion I write letters to God. And I expect God to write back.

An older woman taught me this way of praying. A prayerful person herself, she had been a teacher of the hearing-impaired all her life until retirement. One day when I was experiencing another of my spiritual winters (it really was winter outside with eighteen inches of snow on the ground), I complained to her that I just couldn't make myself pray. I had seemed to lose not only the desire but also the will and the discipline to pray in my usual ways. I told her I needed something to jump-start me into another prayer season. She immediately got up from her chair, went to her desk, and retrieved a thick, wire-bound notebook. "You might need to try a new way of reaching out to God. Take a look at this," she replied. "This is how I pray; it might help you."

My friend gave me a notebook filled with letters she wrote to God. I looked at it quickly, embarrassed to read something so intimate and personal. I tried to give it back to her saying, "I've written to God before. It doesn't help me much." She pushed the notebook back. "Take a good look at it. It may be a little different from what you're used to."

When I read her writing in greater depth, I realized that not only had she written her letters to God, but there were responses to her letters. I looked at her curiously. "From your skeptical expression I gather that you don't believe God writes back? You think these responses come from my imagination? I thought so at first too, but then I found myself writing, 'Who do you think created your imagination? Why wouldn't I use your imagination to communicate with you? As long as what you write corresponds to the truth of scripture, you can be confident that I am present to you through your writing.' At least give it a try," she said. "This has become the most important way of praying for me; I feel we communicate in a much more personal, intimate way than in any of the other methods I've used in the past."

Almost convinced, but not quite, I went home and tried it myself. It seemed a little awkward at first. I had written many letters to God in the past but never expected or even asked God to write back to me. I felt a little foolish, but I kept telling myself that my mind, my imagination were God's creations. So I timidly said, "Dear God, if you want to, I'd love it if you'd write back. I'll be your secretary!" And my winter turned to spring!

Reflection

- How do you reach out to God?
- What is your favorite way of praying?
- What do you do in the winters of your spiritual life?
- What do you think of the idea of writing letters to God?
- How does God respond to you through your imagination? How have you experienced Jesus' promise of "I am with you always"?

GATEWAY 6
Redeeming Loss and Suffering

———❧ ෨෨෨ ❧———

I am now rejoicing in my sufferings for your sake,

and in my flesh I am completing

what is lacking in Christ's afflictions

for the sake of his body, that is, the church.

—COLOSSIANS 1:24

JANE

Finding the Gifts of Diminishment

Scripture

"[Jesus] must increase, but I must decrease" (John 3:30).

"My power is made perfect in weakness" (2 Cor. 12:9, NIV).

*I*MAGINE THAT YOU HAVE just written a letter to God, pleading with God to restore to perfect health the ailment or physical loss that bothers you the most, the one that interferes with living a "normal" life more than any other cause of your suffering. For example, imagine that your physician has just told you he cannot improve your macular degeneration and that you can no longer drive due to poor eyesight that will worsen over time. The resulting losses from that diagnosis are enormous. You feel devastated, angry, sad, afraid—the whole gamut of negative emotions. They flood over you as you envision your future life. This is not what you had planned, not the way you want to live out your Last Third!

Now, imagine that God responds to you with this message:
Dear One,
I have gifted you throughout your life with loving people, beautiful vistas, warm comforts, interesting work, and pleasures both great and small. You have known me through these gifts. Perhaps you have loved the gifts more than you have loved me. I totally understand; my creation is wonderful indeed, and I don't fault you for this. Now, however, as you draw closer to the end of your life, I would like you to know me intimately, to sense how deeply I love you before we meet face-to-face.

I want to give you the source of all the gifts you have ever received—the gift of myself. I want you to know me as I am, as

Love itself. And I don't want any other gifts to distract you or entice you away from me, to come between us. I am asking you to interpret the natural diminishments that come with age as a way to shed all the barriers to my love for you. Use this time to prepare yourself to receive the gift of all gifts—joy with me for all eternity. Know that I am with you and will help you in the midst of all your losses and pain, and I will be with you always. Come to me, and be with me.

Love, God

Reflection

- Can you imagine receiving a letter like this from God? What if you received it right after a devastating loss or suffering from a new bout of a painful condition. Do you think you could attempt to interpret the suffering as a way to draw closer to God?
- What would your barriers to doing so be? God does not send suffering. Pain, suffering, and loss are part of the human condition. Some people suffer more in their lives than others, and this often seems unfair. But if you can reinterpret the suffering as an invitation to draw closer to the God who loves you, will it help significantly?
- How do you feel about getting to know God more intimately before you see God face-to-face? Can you develop such an intense desire for this relationship that all of the other things you have lost become less important to you?

JANE

Lessons from Gethsemane (Part 1)

Scripture

They went to a place called Gethsemane; and he said to his disciples, "Sit here while I pray." He took with him Peter and James and John, and began to be distressed and agitated. And he said to them, "I am deeply grieved, even to death; remain here, and keep awake." And going a little farther, he threw himself on the ground and prayed that, if it were possible, the hour might pass from him. He said, "Abba, Father, for you all things are possible; remove this cup from me; yet, not what I want, but what you want." He came and found them sleeping; and he said to Peter, "Simon, are you asleep? Could you not keep awake one hour?" . . . Their eyes were very heavy; and they did not know what to say to him (Mark 14:32-37, 40).

*B*Y HIS EXAMPLE, Jesus instructs us on how to respond to the pain and suffering that comes into our lives. These lessons follow our modern guidelines for good psychological health. Here are the first four of seven lessons:

1. *We do not need to suffer alone.* Jesus asks his best friends to stay with him while he tries to determine the necessity of his consenting to the fate he sees coming. Following his example, we can and should invite and allow family, friends, and caregivers to support us through our ordeal to the extent they are willing to do so.

2. *We don't have to keep our suffering a secret.* We can talk, even complain, about it. Jesus tells his friends that he is "deeply grieved" and allows them to witness his anguish. By asking them to be near and stay awake, he wants them to know

what he is experiencing. We can follow Jesus' example and share our pain with someone. There is no virtue in keeping our pain a secret. However, like the disciples, some people cannot bear to witness our suffering and may actually leave us alone rather than be there for us.

3. *We need to do all that is reasonable to alleviate our suffering.* Jesus does not want to suffer for its own sake. He does not glorify meaningless suffering, and he speaks honestly with his Father about whether the suffering is necessary, whether his mission would best be accomplished in this way. Likewise, we need not wallow in our pain and suffering. We choose whatever is reasonably appropriate to alleviate the situation. If we suffer from hearing loss, rather than just put up with it we try to find a hearing aid that will enable us to hear!

4. *We should allow ourselves to enter into our suffering and to experience it as a part of our life* if it is unavoidable or cannot be alleviated completely. We work through the pain, using whatever we can to help it. We also avoid fleeing from suffering by engaging in harmful behaviors such as self-neglect, misuse of drugs and alcohol, and even suicide. Once Jesus acknowledges this form of suffering as the way to accomplish his mission, after praying to his Father, he enters into it willingly and maintains his dignity. "Again he went away for the second time and prayed, 'My Father, if this cannot pass unless I drink it, your will be done'" (Matt. 26:42).

Reflection

- Were you taught to suffer politely and virtuously in silence? Do you keep your pain a secret from others, even your closest friends, because you don't want to burden them?

- What do you think about Jesus' desire to have his friends nearby?
- What do you think about Jesus' need to consider other options to accomplish his mission?
- Do you allow yourself to explore all the ways you might lessen your suffering? Have people ever called you a martyr for the way you handle your suffering?

Lessons from Gethsemane (Part 2)

Scripture

"Do you think that I cannot appeal to my Father, and he will at once send me more than twelve legions of angels? But how then would the scriptures be fulfilled, which say it must happen in this way?" (Matt. 26:53-54).

 *J*ESUS TEACHES US HOW to deal with our own suffering:

5. *We can assign meaning to our suffering.* We don't glorify suffering, because suffering is always painful—and God does not send us suffering. However it does not need to be meaningless. We can come to an understanding of it, enter into it, and endure it as part of our personal experience, our unique history. We can affirm its role in shaping us as human beings. We can choose to view suffering as a source of growth, of empathy with the suffering of others, or as a time of personal testing. The more positive the meaning we ascribe to our pain, the better able we are to cope with it.

    After accepting its inevitability and entering into his suffering, Jesus ascribes meaning to it: he is doing the will of the Father, and he is fulfilling the prophecy of the Suffering Servant writings. "All this has taken place, so that the scriptures of the prophets may be fulfilled" (Matt. 26:56).

6. *We can be assured that God never abandons us, even when we don't feel God's presence.* Any severe or chronic pain and suffering, including anxiety and depression, can potentially blot out feelings of confidence that God is a loving God— or even that God exists. We may find ourselves tempted

to believe that God has stopped loving us. Pain, whether physical or psychological, often overwhelms the limbic system of the brain where spiritual feelings are focused. Suffering can eradicate feelings of connectedness and of being loved by God and others. This natural experience can happen to anyone, no matter how devout. Jesus' words from the cross may indicate his experience of spiritual desolation. "About three o'clock Jesus cried with a loud voice, . . . 'My God, my God, why have you forsaken me?'" (Matthew 27:46). Even though he feels that his Father has abandoned him, Jesus refuses to be disconnected from God; the fact that he challenges the Father keeps him from despair. (And it is always acceptable for us to challenge God as well.) Jesus is being asked to live in pure faith, just as many of us have to do at various times of our lives. This sense of abandonment by God can be the most intense suffering of all.

7. *Our suffering energy can be beneficial, redemptive, for others.* Just as his suffering redeems all humankind, our suffering can be redemptive as well. We receive the invitation to imitate Jesus' way of suffering every time pain and suffering come into our own lives. How? By interpreting our suffering as energy for use by the human community and by offering this energy to God, we unite our pain with that of Christ. He can then transform our pain-energy into the gift of loving energy for someone in need. This may be the greatest of Jesus' gifts to us: the transformation of human suffering into love.

Reflection

- How do you handle your suffering? Have you ever ascribed meaning to it? Has it ever been a source of growth, empathy, or a time of testing?

- Picture yourself as Peter, James, or John in the garden of Gethsemane. What do you see? feel? hear?
- Do you believe that you would have been able to stay awake for Jesus?
- When have you resisted visiting a friend in a nursing home or a friend with Alzheimer's disease or cancer because you couldn't bear to see them in such a condition? Because you preferred to remember them as they were when they were well? When were you unable to "stay awake" to a friend's suffering?

JANE

Dedicate Pain and Suffering to Help Others

Scripture

I am now rejoicing in my sufferings for your sake, and in my flesh I am completing what is lacking in Christ's afflictions for the sake of his body, that is, the church (Col. 1:24).

How do you plan to serve God when you become frail? Have you thought about it? Before the discovery of antibiotics and the medical marvels that have ensued, most people either died suddenly or fairly quickly due to illness or injury. The term *death due to natural causes* was common. You rarely hear it anymore. Now we can linger for years as we manage life with chronic debilitating diseases. People who spent their lives working actively and generously for God find themselves feeling they have no way to serve. Over the past thirty-one years as a clinical gerontologist, I have heard so many people who in that situation say to me, "Why doesn't God take me? I'm of no use to anyone any longer!" Often they are told, "Well, at least you have the time to pray now. We need your prayers." Unfortunately, when we experience great physical or emotional pain or suffering, we rarely have the stamina to pray. Even prayer becomes difficult.

But even this situation conveys good news! No matter how weak or ill we are, we can still serve God by following the example of Jesus who suffered to help us and of Paul who told the Colossians about his suffering for their sake. How can we do this? An old devotional practice invited people to "offer up" their sufferings to Jesus as a kind of intercessory prayer. Jesus would then combine those sufferings with his own for the ongoing salvation of the world. The practice fell into disuse years ago, but I have resurrected and modernized it and teach it wherever and whenever I can. When I was ill with lymphoma and taking chemotherapy and a few months later had to have eye surgery, I practiced it.

Here's how I did it:

- I realized that my pain and suffering used up and also created a lot of energy. (We get tired but also have to do special, energy-generating activities to take care of ourselves when we are ill.)
- I offered this suffering energy to Jesus as a gift.
- Each morning I would choose someone who needed help. I then asked Jesus to accept the energy of my suffering and change it into his love for that person.
- I then spent a minute imagining Jesus sending love and help to that person.
- It needs to be done only once during the day. I have found that even when I couldn't pray, I could practice what I have come to call "dedicated suffering."

Both individuals and groups can employ the practice of dedicated suffering. (See Gateway 7, pages 133–35.)

Reflection

- If, because of physical or emotional health, you could no longer serve God in your current fashion, what would you do? What would be your desired action?
- How can you adapt your work for God to accommodate changes in your physical status or living environment?
- How would you serve God if you were confined to bed and in pain?
- What do you think of the idea of dedicating your suffering as Paul did, for the well-being of someone in need? As odd as it may sound to you, are you willing to give it a try?

Remember, you are not asking Jesus to take away your pain; you are asking him to use it to help someone else. Dedicated suffering can be the ministry to which you might be called now or in the future!

- Can you imagine if all the elderly, sick people in the world were to offer their suffering for the well-being of the world, what a change for the good might occur?

JANE

AGING: A NATURAL MONASTERY?

Scripture

"Very truly, I tell you, unless a grain of wheat falls into the earth and dies, it remains just a single grain; but if it dies, it bears much fruit. Those who love their life lose it, and those who hate their life in this world will keep it for eternal life" (John 12:24-25).

"If you wish to be perfect, go, sell your possessions, and give the money to the poor, and you will have treasure in heaven; then come, follow me. (Matt. 19:21).

OUR PRIMARY PURPOSE here on earth is to be able to say, "It is no longer I who live, but it is Christ who lives in me." It takes a long life to arrive at that spiritual state—the state of being a permanent Christ-gift to others. Some people take this aim so seriously that they devote their lives to arriving at this gift. We call these people monks or nuns. Most of them live in monasteries. I believe that old age, the Last Third, is potentially a natural monastery that we all enter, whether we like it or not. And only we can choose to take advantage of the spiritual benefits of such a monastery.

What is a monastery, and why do reasonable adults choose to withdraw from the legitimate pleasures of secular society? How does later life resemble a monastery? First, monasteries are not uniquely Christian communities. For thousands of years men and women of various religious backgrounds have experienced the call to devote their lives to what lies beyond them. Supposedly, Christian monasticism originated with the life of Anthony, who, around 266 CE, withdrew to the desert to seek God in solitude. He lived for twenty years without seeing another person. Would-be disciples came to live in community around him, begging for his spiritual guidance. He emerged for six years to instruct and organize this group of ascetics. By the fourth century CE, the monastic way of life came into full bloom and exists even today.

Why would persons want to retire to a monastery? They make that choice for the following reasons: (1) to devote their total living experience to God; (2) to live with fewer distractions from the good (and not-so-good) things of the secular world; (3) to have more time for community prayer and solitude with God; (4) to have the support of like-minded others; (5) to help God repair the world through the disciplines of prayer, self-denial, and redemptive suffering; (6) to bear witness to a radically different model of productivity.

How does the monastic life enable persons to engage in these objectives? Monastic life requires monks to live in a community of people not of their own choosing—people they may not naturally desire to spend time with, have nothing but God in common with, and/or may even dislike! Monastic life enables monks to lead lives of social marginalization and identification with the world's poor. Monks take the following vows: (1) The vow of poverty requires life in common with little privacy, simplicity of food and relinquishment of concern for taste, satiety and the freedom to choose favorite foods, giving up ownership of personal property, and the enjoyment of physical comforts. (2) The vow of celibacy/chastity requires that persons give up sexual activity, the joy of having a spouse and children, and the company of intimate friends. (3) The vow of stability requires persons to stay in one setting for the rest of their life. (4) The vow of obedience requires obedience to the authority of the abbot or superior (without giving up personal conscience) and relinquishment of control over personal time.

What happens naturally in later life that corresponds with life in a monastery? The above lifestyle and practices of professional religious life closely resemble the sensory, interpersonal, psychological, and material losses of later life. For example, many in late life experience the following: (1) personal, special relationships become fewer or even nonexistent due to death, relocation, sensory losses, and illness; (2) beloved property must be relinquished, especially when moving to a retirement home; (3) enjoyment of physical comforts and pleasures is diminished due to dietary restrictions, inability to digest foods, chronic pain; (4) obedience is required to the authority of the MD, RN, insurance plans, and oversolicitous children; (5) especially in nursing homes persons face loss of many freedoms: lack of control of time, diminished ability to change location, lack of privacy, loss of individuality, and social marginalization.

Younger people report they feel "called" by God to life in the monastery. Perhaps God has seen fit to wean those of us in the Last Third of life and facing death from overattachment to the world. Perhaps God is preparing us for the gift of a deeper, stronger, more intimate relationship with Love itself. Then we also can say, at the end of our lives, "It is no longer I who live, but it is Christ who lives in me."

Reflection

- How might reconceptualizing the losses of late life as a natural monastery help you?
- What would your "'natural monastery'" be like?

Richard

So Many Losses

Scripture

Job again took up his discourse and said:
"O, that I were as in the months of old,
as in the days when God watched over me;
when his lamp shone over my head,
 and by his light I walked through darkness;
when I was in my prime" (Job 29:1-4).

Losses occur throughout life, but they come at a faster pace in the Last Third of life. Loss of home, friends, work, and health hit us in rapid succession. We can identify with the patriarch Job, who suffered loss after loss, including children and health. So, like Job we yearn for the years when we were in our prime. But the years take their toll, and our bodies grow frailer with every passing day. Our renewed spirits may buoy us, but we cannot stop the inevitable weaknesses of older age.

Two of the great losses come in the loss of mobility and loss of memory. Having to use a cane has slowed me down considerably. I can only drive a few blocks from our home, so I gave my car to my grandson. I miss the freedom of driving to bookstores or taking short trips. I rely on my wife for transportation or find myself at the mercy of others who take me where I want to go. However, I have learned dependence and freedom from the need of being in control. Furthermore, not burdened with the stress of driving, I now enjoy the scenery.

An old saying states, "Of all the things I've lost, I miss my mind the most." If geriatricians are right that 50 percent of persons eighty-five or older will succumb to Alzheimer's disease, I am not far from that frightening possibility. I know that vascular dementia lurks in my genes, and I have had some sporadic attacks, now under control through medication.

I am quite aware of memory loss. Three things I tend to forget: the names of persons I just met, what I did yesterday, and—I can't remember the third thing! We all have noted "senior moments" when we temporarily lose our train of thought. I always had a sharp memory. My friends would chuckle as I rattled off Bible verses and the names of baseball players. Now that ease of recollection has begun to fade.

Neurologists tell us that the brain starts to shrink as we age, and a massive number of brain cells die. No wonder it takes longer to learn, retain, and recall information in our later years. Mild cognitive impairment occurs as we age, but that does not mean we will develop Alzheimer's disease. In fact, studies show that we can grow new brain cells every day.[1] Despite the rhetoric that older persons' mental life declines, we can maintain a vigorous mental life through the whole life span. It can actually peak in late life. So I work on training my brain[2] by reading, doing crossword puzzles, attempting new skills. Even loss of mobility and memory can be transformed by "the renewing of our mind" (Rom. 12:2, AP).

Reflection

Read the poem by John C. Morgan.

Love

Only old people with wrinkles and arthritis
know about love.
It's all worth saving
when everything else is gone.
Grown taut by disappointments,

the body awaits the end
and can no longer melt under lover's heat.
Only dying persons find each day
a lifetime,
for that is all that's worth finding.
Facing death makes love everything.[3]

- How does this poem strike you? Does it seem too negative or does it strike you as realistic?
- What about its description of our bodies as they age rings true with you?
- What older persons does it bring to your mind? Do you agree that "only old people . . . know about love"?

[1]"Landmark discoveries by Fred Gage, PhD, at the Salk Institute for Biological Studies in California, and by other researchers showed that thousands of neurons are born in the brain daily, primarily in the hippocampus, a learning and memory region. The process is called neurogenesis."

[2]Jean Carper, *100 Simple Things You Can Do to Prevent Alzheimer's and Age-Related Memory Loss* (New York: Little, Brown and Company, 2010), 46.

[3]John Crossley Morgan, "Love," in *Thin Places* (Eugene, OR: Resource Publications, 2009), 24.

RICHARD

My Friends—They're All Gone

Scripture

I grieve for you, Jonathan my brother;
  you were very dear to me.
Your love for me was wonderful (2 Sam. 1:26, NIV).

1 LISTENED PATIENTLY to the lament of a ninety-year-old woman as she responded to news of a death in our community. "They're all gone," she said sadly. "I've lived so long, and so many friends have died; there won't be anyone at my funeral." I live in a community where death visits almost weekly. When we reach the Last Third of life, the number of friends becomes fewer. Death becomes the great detractor, as it takes away people we love. Our world narrows, and we seem to live in a world all our own.

Bill, a close friend, lived in an apartment above my wife and me. I often visited him to talk and to watch Duke basketball. He would stare out his window and admire the big oak tree. When he died, all I could think about was a line from Edwin Markham's epic poem "Lincoln, Man of the People": He left behind a "lonesome place against the sky." Even now I stare at that tree and mourn Bill's loss. Disruptive moments come in the loss of friends or family members. In the biblical tradition, life entails both loss and gain, death and resurrection.

Some residents build a protective wall around themselves and refuse to develop close friendships. They tell me, "I just can't stand to lose so many friends here. I keep my distance." I do get close to other residents and mourn their loss, which diminishes me. However, the loss of friends can transform our lives. Their death reminds us that life is short, and each day is precious. Every awakening offers an opportunity to make the day count. We consciously ignore little irritants and avoid trivialities. We transform loss by cherishing each day.

The loss of friends means we treasure their memories. I feel sure that David never forgot Jonathan's friendship. Jonathan's father, King Saul, consumed by jealousy and torn by moods of depression and paranoia, viewed David as a threat to his throne and tried to kill him. Repeatedly Jonathan had sided against Saul and was there to warn David and help him escape. These memories would linger and remind David of a friendship that death could not destroy.

Our monthly memorial services here give the community members an opportunity not only to mourn but to celebrate the lives of those we have loved long since. The words of W. B. Yeats strike a chord with me, "Think where man's glory most begins and ends, / And say my glory was I had such friends." ("The Municipal Gallery Revisited")

Reflection
- Take a few moments in a quiet place to remember family and friends who have died. What are your happiest memories of these people?
- How did they contribute to your life?
- As you grieve their loss, offer prayers of thanksgiving for their lives.

GATEWAY 7
Leaving a Legacy

———⟡———

The time of my departure has come. I have fought the good fight,
I have finished the race, I have kept the faith.

—2 TIMOTHY 4:6-7

RICHARD

How Do You Want to Be Remembered?

Scripture

"Do not store up for yourselves treasures on earth, where
moth and rust consume and where thieves break in and steal;
but store up for yourselves treasures in heaven, where neither
moth nor rust consumes and where thieves do not break in
and steal. For where your treasure is, there your heart will be
also" (Matt. 6:19-21).

$\mathcal{L}$AST YEAR OUR FRIEND and next-door neighbor Nancy was
found dead in her apartment. It happened suddenly and came as
a shock. Each person's death in this community diminishes me,
but I felt deeply Nancy's loss. Her tireless work at Children's Hospital in Pittsburgh and her many acts of kindness to the people of
this community became her legacy. She left a trail of good deeds
that will linger for years.

What kind of legacy do you want to leave for your family and
friends when you die? Ordinarily, leaving a legacy implies the dis-
tribution of money and property to heirs according to the terms
described in a legal document, known as a will. However, I will
have few material things and no stock portfolio to leave my children. When my wife and I moved to this retirement community,
we downsized most of our possessions. The high cost of living
here has stretched our finances to the limit. But I will have a treasure not measured by material standards to leave my family: my
life. Every life leaves a legacy, and right now I am working on the
legacy I plan to leave.

Jesus' compelling words about storing up "treasures in heaven" remind us that all we will take into the next world and all we will leave our family is our values, life lessons, and wisdom. This legacy extends far beyond our fiscal worth. Our legacy does not end the day we die. It becomes the crowning moment of the life we leave behind.

Leaving a legacy of faith becomes a powerful spiritual reality because it validates our lives. How will future generations remember us? By snapshots in faded photo albums? By fleeting memories gathered at our memorial service? By a few words in an obituary or carved on tombstones? Our real legacy resides in the life we leave behind, the spiritual treasures we have stored in heaven.

Reflection

- What legacy will you leave behind?
- How do you want your family to remember you?
- Have you considered writing a spiritual will, describing your values and beliefs?
- These extended years bless you with time to complete in yourself what has been neglected all these years. To what do you turn your attention?

RICHARD

Connecting with Ancestors

Scripture

Listen to me, you that pursue righteousness,
    you that seek the LORD.
Look to the rock from which you were hewn,
    and to the quarry from which you were dug.
Look to Abraham your father
    and to Sarah who bore you (Isa. 51:1-2).

OFTEN AS WE LIVE in the later years, we grow closer to those who came before us. Our lives began before our birth and will continue through those who follow. When I first "retired," I spent many hours researching my ancestors and could affirm with the psalmist, "I have a goodly heritage." Now that I am much older, parents and grandparents seem much closer. I have the vivid sense of their presence with me. They offer me comfort by letting me know they have gone before and passed into a new life.

My Welsh Celtic tradition speaks of "thin places" where the veil that separates heaven from earth is lifted and we catch a fleeting glimpse of the other world. I sensed a "thin place" as a pilgrim to Tintern Abbey in Wales. At dawn one morning I walked around the deserted abbey, and I could imagine monks rising to prepare for yet another day. That morning I found the abbey deserted and heard no sounds except a small choir of birds announcing the sun's resurrection. Yet, the veil that separates the moment to come from what lies beyond seemed to open for me.

That veil also becomes thin at times of dying. My sister, dying with cancer, told me that she had "seen" our parents and grandparents shortly before her death. Some native traditions claim that ancestor spirits appear to dying persons as guides to the other world.

In her novel *The Lovely Bones*, Alice Sebold notes that heaven is a place from which those who have died can look down on the living and observe them. Many times I have felt the closeness with those whom I have loved long since. Whenever I hear the Irish melody "Danny Boy," my father's presence becomes real, since he sang that song so many times. I believe our ancestors see us now; we cannot see them, although at times we sense their presence.

I often use the words of an Inuit legend at memorial services and name those whom we remember: "Perhaps they are not the stars, but rather openings in heaven where the love of our lost ones pours through and shines down upon us to let us know they are happy."

As we leave our legacy for generations to come, we do so with gratitude for those who went before us. They live undiminished in us and will live on, united with us and our descendants.

O blest communion, fellowship divine!
We feebly struggle, they in glory shine;
Yet all are one in Thee, for all are Thine.
—William Walsham How, "For All the Saints"

Reflection

- How do you honor your ancestors?
- Have you listened to their stories and recorded them?
- What qualities in your ancestors' legacy live on in you?

Richard

My Legacy: Faith at the End of Life

Scripture

The time of my departure has come. I have fought the good fight, I have finished the race, I have kept the faith (2 Tim. 4:6-7).

In the movie *About Schmidt*, Jack Nicholson portrays Warren Schmidt, a sixty-six-year-old man who is forced to deal with lingering regrets about his life as he enters retirement. Shortly after his wife dies, his dreams die as well. He says, "Relatively soon, I will die. . . . Once I am dead and everyone who knew me dies too, it will be as though I never existed. What difference has my life made to anyone? None that I can think of. None at all."

As I think about my legacy, I recall the words Martin Luther King Jr. spoke two months before his death: "I'd like somebody to mention that day that Martin Luther King, Jr., tried to give his life serving others. . . . tried to love somebody."[1]

A quote attributed (although inaccurately) to Ralph Waldo Emerson summarized his legacy this way, "To leave the world a bit better, whether by a healthy child, a garden patch or a redeemed social condition; to know even one life has breathed easier because you have lived. This is to have succeeded."

I believe my legacy shines forth in the countless number of people I have helped, standing with them and embracing them with God's unconditional love. As I replay my life, I remember young and old, whose lives I touched and helped to find God's grace. I worked for racial justice in colleges and churches, at the cost of losing a professorship and some members of churches I served. I worked all my life for the poorest, sickest, and oldest of our society, so often bypassed by those who demanded their rights rather than what was right. My legacy will be my children and grandchildren whom I have loved all my life and whom I have tried to keep aware of my love and support.

My legacy is found in the words of this book that the Last Third of life need not be a time of decline and despair. Despite the inevitable chronic illnesses that come in the Last Third of life, our inner spirit can be renewed daily. We can find joy at the end of life and affirm Jesus' words that the good wine is kept until the end.

Reflection

- In a book written shortly before his death from cancer, Carnegie Mellon Professor Randy Pausch delivered his last lecture, which has been preserved in his book by that name. He wanted to put himself in a bottle that would one day wash up on shore for his children. Imagine you were a college professor giving his or her last lecture before retirement. What would you say?
- Or, if you were retiring from a career, what would you say at a retirement celebration in your honor?

[1]Clayborne Carson and Peter Holloran, eds., *A Knock at Midnight: Inspiration from the Great Sermons of Reverend Martin Luther King, Jr.* (New York: Warner Books, 1998), 185.

JANE

The Power of Loving-kindness

Scripture

[A capable wife] opens her mouth with wisdom,
    and the teaching of kindness is on her tongue
(Prov. 31:26).

SINGLE ALL HER LIFE, Kate had been a social worker for forty years, avidly involved in improving the well-being of foster children. Known for her keen intelligence, quick wit, and fiercely independent spirit, she did not take kindly to the lack of control she experienced as a resident of a (very expensive) nursing home. A mutual friend told me of visiting her one afternoon, only to find her room empty. As she approached the nurses' station to ask Kate's whereabouts, she overheard a conversation between two of the aides: "Could you finish Kate's shower for me? If she insults me one more time, I don't know if I'll be able to hold it together. I just want to tell her off—she is such a nasty woman. No wonder she stayed single all her life. Who would want to live with her? Can you even imagine being her child? Judy is with her now but can't stay. You get along with her better than I do. Would you finish the job, please?" The friend said she hastily returned to Kate's room and left a small gift along with a note saying that she would visit another time.

As the two of us discussed Kate and her living situation, we talked about the transformation of our friend from a fun-loving, high-spirited, generous woman with lots of friends into a sour, demanding, negative person. Instead of using her quick wit to generate laughter, she had allowed her tongue to become sharp and critical of everyone who cared for her, even her friends. It had come to the point that we all dreaded our obligatory visits to her. When one of us didn't visit at least once a week, she'd call and leave voice messages on our phones with comments like, "So what am I now, chopped liver? I can't amuse you, so you're dropping me? A fine, fair-weather friend you are!" and then she'd slam the phone down. Friends were finding it more and more difficult to visit.

Unfortunately, transformation from nice to nasty often occurs in later life, and relocation to an institutional setting doesn't necessarily cause it. When we experience the challenges of late life, especially the physical insults of the Last Third, we can all too easily settle into a habit of seeing life as a glass half full—and punishing those around us for it. But we need to ask ourselves two questions: Is this the way we want to be remembered? Is this the example of how to deal with the blows of late life that we want to leave as a legacy to those who will outlive us?

How can we combat a growing tendency to bitterness and nastiness in our final years when everything is taken away from us? What can we do to change a nursing home aide's response from "She was so mean, I'm not sorry she's gone!" to "She was the kindest person I have ever met. I will miss her"? I think developing the attitude and behavior of loving-kindness is the key. Anyone in any condition can give this legacy.

Webster's defines *kindness* as a "habit of goodwill, affection. Someone who is kind is sympathetic, friendly, tenderhearted, gentle, generous." Loving-kindness goes even farther. Loving-kindness, a translation of the Hebrew word *hesed*, refers to God's covenantal relationship with God's people. While kindness is a well-mannered way of behaving, loving-kindness goes above and beyond niceties. It implies a recognition that we are all in it together and can't survive without one another. It is characterized not only by goodwill but by a readiness to forgive, to refuse to take offense, to go beyond the minimal duty toward neighbor. This quality of being is motivated by love rather than mere good manners. I pray that if I find myself in need of total care, whether at home or in a nursing home, I can serve as an instrument of God's loving-kindness to everyone who has to care for me. I want to exemplify how this way of being can change the quality of life for all concerned. I have plenty of work to do on myself!

Reflection

- How do you feel when someone speaks sharply to you, is critical, negative, or downright nasty?
- How do you feel when someone has gone out of the way to be kind?
- When have you been the recipient of someone's loving-kindness? How did that affect you?
- If you were in Kate's situation, how might you transform an unwanted life situation into one that reveals God's loving-kindness? If not, what might help you develop this quality?

JANE

My Legacy: Dedicated Suffering

Scripture

It makes me happy to be suffering for you now, and in my own body to make up all the hardships that still have to be undergone by Christ for the sake of his body, the Church (COL. 1:24, NJB).

EVER SINCE SUCCESSFULLY completing chemotherapy for lymphoma, I have had a CT scan every three months to determine whether I am still in remission. I usually have the CT scan on a Thursday and meet with my oncologist the following Tuesday to discuss the results. About two weeks prior to the scan, anxiety sets in. I start noticing little changes in my body that might indicate the recurrence of the cancer. When that happens I (yet again) begin to prepare for my dying process. That means that I take stock of my life since the last CT to determine if I am "on track" with the legacy I want to leave.

I chose my legacy suddenly in April 2009, while in the hospital, just after being told that I was suffering from stage 4.5, diffuse, B-cell, non-Hodgkin's lymphoma. My husband, Ron, called our two pastors, Fr. Roy Stiles (Roman Catholic) and Rev. Bill Vanderford (United Methodist) to attend to my spiritual needs. In an ecumenical anointing service at my bedside, Fr. Roy, Rev. Bill, his wife Diane, and Ron prayed for my spiritual well-being and healing. Fr. Roy asked each person what his or her personal prayer was for me. Then he asked me what my prayer was for myself. That request surprised me, and I took a moment to think about it. I asked God what gift I could give, what legacy I might leave during the time I had left on earth. Then without hesitation I replied, "I would like to have some time to play with Ron, and I would like to spend the rest of my time teaching 'dedicated suffering' to as many people as I possibly can." (I said I wanted time to play with Ron because I had been so tied up with work responsibilities for the twenty-seven years we'd been married that I had neglected to take time to savor the sheer joy of spending time with this wonderful man. I didn't want to die without trying to make up for that!)

As I mentioned in an earlier chapter, I discovered my "call," which will become my legacy—dedicated suffering—about fifteen years ago. At the time I was trying to find a way to help suffering older adults find spiritual meaning for their lives. Dedicated suffering is one way Jesus has taught us to transform our pain and suffering into a gift of love for other people in need. It is based on Paul's enigmatic statement about being happy to suffer for the Colossians, which teaches that our own suffering, when combined with the sufferings of Christ, can also be redemptive. Long a devotional practice in the Catholic church of "offering up" one's sufferings, it had gone out of ecclesial style many years ago.

As a gerontologist working with older adults in ongoing pain and suffering, I have resurrected it, modernized it, renamed it (from "redemptive" to "intercessory" to "dedicated" suffering) and teach it wherever, whenever, and to whomever I have the opportunity. I explained earlier how to practice dedicated suffering as an individual. For a group of two or more, sitting in a circle, follow this process: (1) Going around the circle, each person takes a turn to state in only one or two sentences his or her predominant physical, psychological, or social suffering. (2) When all have spoken, the group discusses and decides who or what cause (outside of the group) needs help. (3) The group offers the energy from their combined suffering to Christ, prayerfully asking him to transform it into loving-kindness for the chosen person. (4) The group takes one minute to visualize the Holy Spirit offering Christ's loving-kindness to the person. This is very much like intercessory prayer but uses suffering as prayer because people who suffer often lament that they cannot pray. In this way they can participate in the ongoing welfare of Christ's community. I hope to have many years to share the practice of dedicated suffering; but if I don't, I hope this legacy will be strong enough to continue!

Reflection

- Have you ever thought about leaving a spiritual legacy? Have you identified your legacy?
- What might you give to the world that you would never have been able to leave if you had not received the gift of long life?
- Do you need help from a spiritual companion or mentor to decide upon a legacy?

RICHARD

Letter to Grandchildren

Scripture

The good leave an inheritance to their children's children
(PROV. 13:22).

OF ALL MY LIFE'S treasures, none is greater than our ten grandchildren. They are scattered across the four corners of the country. I edit a grandchildren's newsletter, *The Messenger*, so they can connect with one another and I can keep up with them. I realize that I am writing to people who probably will not read this letter now. However, perhaps they will read it later and remember me. Because of these grandchildren and their children the earth will not be as if I never walked on it.

Dear Grandchildren:

I have no right to tell you what to think or how to live, but I have every right and duty to tell you my values and hopes for you:

That you will remember the values by which I lived.
- Treat others as you would like to be treated.
- Be kind to everyone, especially the poor, the weak, and the outsider.
- Keep learning all your life, for the life of the mind is the service of God.

That you will remember my faith and find one of your own.
- Discover your own faith through doubt and inquiry.
- Allow your faith to support you when life becomes difficult; faith will help you get through it.
- Keep the inner life strong; don't let materialism take it away.

That you will cherish and love another person as your soul mate.
- Find a partner who will be your companion throughout life.
- Value the importance of close friends.

That you will discover and flourish in your own career.
- Find where your deepest joy and the needs of the world meet.
- Explore many options, but choose the right career for you.

That you will find joy in life.
- Don't take yourself too seriously. Lighten up; laugh a lot. Take hikes in the mountains, walk the beaches. Enjoy sunsets, flowers, and stars at night.
- Know that your families will love you unconditionally and you reside in the embrace of a God who loves you as you are.

Your grandfather,
Gramps

Reflection
- Write a letter to your grandchildren that expresses your values, beliefs, and wishes for them.
- If you have no grandchildren, write a letter to children or someone in the next generation.

RICHARD

The Final Gateway

Scripture

Open to me the gates of righteousness,
> that I may enter through them.

. . . .

This is the gate of the LORD;
> the righteous shall enter through it (Ps. 118:19-20).

In this book, Jane and I have written about seven gateways to spiritual growth in the Last Third of life. One final gateway, which all must enter sooner or later, is that of death. I am both scared and curious about my death and what lies beyond. When we face death we feel like foreigners who don't know the language. The gateways guard their secrets well, and we can only wonder what lies beyond that final gate. Even those who have had near-death experiences don't really know. Many claim to have seen a light and a tunnel, but some who study this phenomenon say that it has more to do with the release of chemicals in the brain than life after death. All we have are hints and guesses as we face this mystery.

Rossiter Worthington Raymond once wrote, "Death is only a horizon; and a horizon is nothing save the limit of our sight." The writer of First John described it this way, "Beloved, we are God's children now; what we will be has not yet been revealed. What we do know is this: when he is revealed, we will be like him, for we will see him as he is" (3:2).

I hope that death is a homecoming where our loved ones wait for us and welcome us home. I imagine them saying, "They're here," as the gates open and the celebration begins. There will be food and laughter and stories from our lives. Despite the unknown, we can feel assured that we will return to the home we never left. So there is nothing to fear.

Yet all our thoughts are speculations. So we put our trust in Jesus' words to his disciples the night before his death: "Do not let your hearts be troubled. Believe in God, believe also in me. In my Father's house there are many dwelling places" (John 14:1-2). I hold to these words and for the rest am totally uncommitted.

The book of Revelation closes with an imaginative vision (Rev. 22:1-5): a city whose gates remain open and where it is always light. By faith we will pass through that open gate to that Eternal Light.

Reflection

- Contemplate the words of Natalie Sleeth's "Hymn of Promise." Silently remember your loved ones who have died and then meditate on your own death.

> In the bulb there is a flower; in the seed,
> an apple tree;
> in cocoons, a hidden promise: butterflies
> will soon be free!
> In the cold and snow of winter
> there's a spring that waits to be,
> unrevealed until its season,
> something God alone can see.
>
> There's a song in every silence
> seeking word and melody;
> there's a dawn in every darkness,
> bringing hope to you and me.
> From the past will come the future;
> what it holds, a mystery,

unrevealed until its season,
something God alone can see.

In our end is our beginning; in our time,
infinity;
in our doubt there is believing,
in our life, eternity.
In our death, a resurrection;
at the last, a victory,
unrevealed until its season,
something God alone can see.

Suggested Reading

Agronin, Marc E. *How We Age: A Doctor's Journey into the Heart of Growing Old.* Philadephia, PA: Da Capo Press, 2011.

Arrien, Angeles. *The Second Half of Life: Opening the Eight Gates of Wisdom.* Louisville, CO: Sounds True, 2007.

Chittister, Joan. *The Gift of Years: Growing Older Gracefully.* New York: BlueBridge Books, 2008.

Dass, Ram. *Still Here: Embracing Aging, Changing and Dying.* New York: Riverhead Books/Penguin, 2001.

Hollis, James. *Finding Meaning in the Second Half of Life: How to Finally, Really Grow Up.* New York: Gotham Books/Penguin, 2006.

Jacoby, Susan. *Never Say Die: The Myth and Marketing of the New Old Age.* New York: Pantheon Books/Knopf Doubleday, 2011.

Morgan, Richard. *Fire in the Soul: A Prayerbook for the Later Years.* Nashville, TN: Upper Room Books, 2000.

Morgan, Richard L., Howard C. Morgan, and John C. Morgan. *Dear Brothers: Letters Facing Death.* Eugene, OR: Wipf and Stock Publishers, 2009.

Plotkin, Bill. *Nature and the Human Soul: Cultivating Wholeness and Community in a Fragmented World.* Novato, CA: New World Library, 2007.

Rohr, Richard. *Falling Upward: A Spirituality for the Two Halves of Life.* San Francisco, CA: Jossey-Bass/Wiley, 2011.

Sherman, Edmund. *Contemplative Aging: A Way of Being in Later Life.* New York: Gordian Knot Books/Richard Altschuler and Associates, 2010.

Thibault, Jane Marie. *10 Gospel Promises for Later Life.* Nashville, TN: Upper Room Books, 2004.

About the Authors

JANE MARIE THIBAULT is a gerontologist and emerita clinical professor in the Department of Family and Geriatric Medicine, School of Medicine, University of Louisville, Kentucky, where she taught for thirty-one years. She also has served as an adjunct faculty member for the Louisville Presbyterian Theological Seminary and is currently a consultant for aging issues, specializing in the spiritual dimensions of aging.

Jane is the author of several journal articles and books, including *Understanding Religious and Spiritual Aspects of Human Service Practice, A Deepening Love Affair: The Gift of God in Later Life; 10 Gospel Promises for Later Life*, and *No Act of Love Is Ever Wasted: The Spirituality of Caring for Persons with Dementia*. A trained spiritual director, she provides spiritual direction, workshops, and retreats for senior adults and their caregivers. She is married to Ronald Fryrear.

RICHARD L. MORGAN lives in a retirement community near Pittsburgh, Pennsylvania, where he continues writing and caring for persons with dementia and their caregivers. He holds degrees from Davidson College, an MA in Counseling from Wake Forest University, and three degrees from Union Presbyterian Seminary, including a PhD.

Dick is a national leader on issues of aging and spiritual autobiography. He has written twenty books, including *Remembering Your Story: A Guide to Spiritual Autobiography* and *Settling In: My First Year in a Retirement Community*. He is married to Alice Ann Morgan. He may be reached at his Web site: http://richardmorganauthor.com where he writes a weekly blog, "View from Eighty."

CPSIA information can be obtained at www.ICGtesting.com
Printed in the USA
LVOW04s1242230914

405430LV00005B/12/P